Manipulation

Learn To Spot Manipulation As An Empath

Improve Your Emotional Intelligence In Work And Life

Table of Contents

This page has been intentionally left blank

Introduction

Do you find yourself talking and sharing way too much with certain people? If yes, then you might be getting attacked by manipulators in your life. Manipulators have the ability to make you share your emotional strengths and weaknesses. They have their tactics, which doesn't allow you to protect your emotional side.

People surrounded with manipulators often struggle to find self-confidence. If you don't know how manipulation works, manipulators can shake your life completely. You feel as if you are in debt of them. They control your life, your emotions, and your actions. People who face manipulation feel betrayed and confused in life. Manipulators have the capability to twist realities and make you see what they want; hence, your ability to understand your environment gets corrupted. You start making wrong decisions that ruin your life, but benefits your manipulator. It is a state of psychological and emotional slavery, which you need to break as soon as possible.

What Problems Do You Face At Work And In General Life?

Manipulation is different than social influence. Every person tries to understand other people in order to make stronger relationships; however, manipulators don't think that way. They observe and control people to exploit them. You are nothing but a tool for them. You end up serving a purpose for a manipulator without even knowing it.

- Your self-esteem is attacked by people at your workplace.

- People use your caring nature and then leave you alone.

- You are losing confidence in people because of a few in your life.

- You feel trapped in your family and feel exploited by family members.

- You never say "no" to a certain person in your life.

- You are facing other people's problems and not able to cope.

- Your workplace has become a negative environment for you.

- You feel violated mentally, emotionally and physically.

All these problems and more are possible if you are not ready to tackle manipulators. Not knowing about manipulators makes you vulnerable. Also, you have to understand your emotions, passions, psychology, and habits. A healthy life is the one that is free from manipulation.

What Will This Book Do For You?

When manipulators are out there trying to learn and use you, it is important that you understand their methods. There are many types of manipulations and different kinds of manipulators out there. They all use different methods and target different emotions or psychological state of people. This book will allow you to understand how manipulation works. You will learn to spot manipulative tactics and methods to avoid manipulation.

This book explains how manipulators work in a workplace, in a relationship or in other life settings people indulge in, generally. You will learn how to have conversations with a manipulator and how to not fall for their lies and deceptions.

Apart from knowing how manipulation works, you will find solutions to all the problems mentioned above. This book will also allow you to understand your own emotional, psychological and mental state and remove all vulnerabilities.

Emotional and social awareness is extremely important if you want to live a psychologically healthy life. You can have deep, hidden emotional issues affecting your habits today. This book has a comprehensive approach to how to deal with manipulation and improve your social and self-awareness. You will learn to manage your emotions and open up to the right people. Becoming a self-confident person and dealing with your emotional issues is the way to find true happiness.

With complete self-awareness and social awareness, you hold the steering wheel of your own life; hence, no manipulator can find any room to control your actions.

Let's begin the most important journey of your life!

CHAPTER 1 - What Is Manipulation?

Manipulation is using people's emotions and behavioral traits deliberately to obtain what is desired. Manipulators use their ability to understand others and get what they want by using trickery, misdirection, persuasion, charm, and coaxing.

In the mind of a manipulator, he or she thinks, "I have the ability to change people's behavior and let them give me what I want." Skilled manipulators can even come out of a situation when they get caught trying to use other people to their advantage.

A manipulator has a tendency to create a certain level of strain in a situation. They use multiple techniques to mold their personality according to their goals. A manipulator can make you feel on top of the world, or the worst person on this planet. It all depends on how that manipulator wants you to act.

Manipulation, as a concept, involves two parties. One is the manipulator and the other is manipulated. While manipulators are extremely aware of their surroundings, some personalities tend to ignore that. People, who are emotionally vulnerable or don't have a clear mindset, tend to get manipulated.

Generally speaking, everyone manipulates without knowing. Lying or hiding the complete story are a few common ways of manipulation; however, manipulators live these tactics as the way of their lives. They use various tactics as their tools to fool you into doing what they want.

That's why you need to understand all types of manipulation and more importantly, learn how to address it positively in different aspects of your life.

Different Types of Manipulation

If you aren't aware enough, manipulators can use many techniques to control you. They change their approach depending on the victim's personality so they first observe you and learn your core personality traits. At the core, you can be a loving person, a lonely person, naïve or too confident.

With personality observation, manipulators create their tactic to attack you. Here are different types of manipulation that you need to become aware of:

1. Hiding the complete story

You can notice this in your office, parties and other conversations taking place around you. There are people who hide certain portions of stories in order to create a diversion. The listener of the story gets to know what the manipulator wants him to know.

What if a colleague in your office tells you how others are bitching about you! It is possible that you are getting half of the side of the story, but if you are unaware of manipulation, this half story can trigger emotions like anger and hatred, and you end up doing something that you regret.

When a manipulator uses a half story, they don't lie. They just avoid telling certain portions so that you see a picture of their creation. The tactic behind this method is to stay on the safe side. If exposed, the manipulator can simply say that he or she has explained nothing but the truth and in doing so, you risk facing humiliation due to your wrong actions.

2. Lying

Generally, people lie when they are scared or want to get out of an unwanted situation, but a manipulator's lie is different. Their lies always have a purpose or an end goal. In fact, they don't even have to plan before lying. They can plan their next lie while having a conversation with you.

Depending on what they want, manipulators can choose different lies to make you their victim. It is a blend of thrill and excitement they feel while trying to play your personality.

3. Love and charm

Narcissistic manipulators use love and charm to control you. This behavior is majorly visible in love relationships between partners. You get hooked and think that your partner loves you the most. They charm and create an illusion of a perfect relationship. These people always want something from you.

When love has built the foundation, the manipulator uses that to control you. They can ask for things, money or just play with your emotions. The goals depend on the personality of the manipulator. Some people have the disorder to love and then hurt their partners. The roots of this behavior lead back to their own previous experiences.

To spot the manipulation of love, you need to notice who is making decisions in your relationship:

• Do you feel afraid of your partner when making a personal choice?

• Has it become your habit to get your partner's approval on everything?

• Are you doing things that you wouldn't do otherwise?

These questions can help you decipher love manipulation in your daily life.

4. Changing behavior frequently

This is different than changing personality traits according to a victim. A manipulator, many times, may showcase a behavioral change towards the same person again and again. Now, you can think of all those people who seem different every time you meet them. This behavior is common in love relationships, and boss and employee relationships as well.

The manipulator wants you to stay malleable and out of balance so, one minute he or she can look happy, and swiftly become angry for no valid reason. However, they make you think that their behavioral switch has a legitimate reason. Your boss can start shouting angrily just for a single typo in your report. Similarly, a manipulative partner can come home with a different mood every day.

We, as humans, understand other people's personalities before socializing. You feel more comfortable around a person who you know well, instead of a stranger, but manipulators use their mood swings to keep you scared and afraid of them. You feel unaware of their personalities and try to please them.

5. Denying accusations

A manipulator can deny things very impressively. If you accuse them of something, they confidently present a believable story. The confidence, combined with an impressive story, makes you believe them.

Denying accusations is the simplest form of manipulation. In fact, this is the first tactic that manipulators use in their early ages. A kid with manipulative tendencies usually denies things with confidence and makes stories to justify their case.

6. Punishments

Punishment is a disciplinary action to control other people's behavior. This is also a manipulation technique that gives your control to a manipulator. Physical violence, shouting, and nagging are the visible techniques of manipulation.

Apart from that, you can also get emotionally punished with the silence of a person or mental abuse. A manipulator can attack your emotional vulnerabilities to make you feel bad. They keep on doing it until you start behaving exactly the way they want. Such manipulation is seen in marriages a lot. One partner uses physical and mental abuse to control the other. Also, you can notice these manipulation symptoms in a parent-kid relationship. A manipulative kid can use the silent treatment to control his or her mother.

7. Blaming for overreaction

Is there a person who makes you feel bad about yourself?! That person can be a manipulator.

Using the blame game allows a manipulator to put you on the

faulty side of every conversation. If you point out their actions, they blame you for overreacting. They say that you are reacting way too much for a very small thing. This way they become the victim and you end up feeling bad about your own actions.

8. Victim targeting

You are the victim, but the accuser makes you defend yourself in front of others. This way, the manipulator masks his or her own wrongdoings by shifting the focus towards you. The manipulator does it all in front of you, but you feel out of control of the situation.

9. Playing a victim

Have you ever helped people whom you never liked as a person? Then it is possible that you were used with this manipulation technique.

Manipulators play victim from time to time to gain compassion and sympathy. Their end goal is always to use you in some way; however, not every victim is a manipulator. Some are genuinely hurt and require your support, but manipulators can use your helping nature to get what they want.

10. Too much positive attention

The corporate world is filled with such manipulators nowadays. People use expensive presents, give money, and praise to lure you towards them. Excessive charm and too much attention are used for people who seek approval and like getting praised. Manipulators judge personalities and give too much attention to satisfy your emotional needs.

Positive attention works if you are emotionally vulnerable. For instance, if you mention "society" before taking every action, it tells a manipulator about your approval-seeking nature. Your high-class dressing sense and money-focused behavior also give signals to manipulators. They start giving you the royal treatment and manipulate in the process.

11. Diversions

Shifting situations and conversations are also manipulation techniques. You feel you know what's going on, but suddenly a person changes the whole picture. If that happens in your life frequently, then there is a manipulator around you. He or she wants you to stay confused, while they get to twist situations in their favor.

When in a group conversation, a manipulator plays the role of a narrator. If a conversation goes against his or her plan, they immediately shift the topic to something else. These manipulators become the kings and queens of office politics.

12. Isolation

Manipulation is difficult when you are consulting your family and friends on the same topic; hence, a manipulator tries everything to isolate you from other people. This doesn't have to be a literal isolation. The manipulator can tell you to keep things a secret from everyone. Once you agree to that, he or she can twist your behavior easily.

Covert and Overt Types of Manipulation

Covert and overt are two major categories of manipulation.

Covert manipulation combines all the invisible techniques of manipulation. You can't see the psychological attacks of an abuser until it's done. This type of manipulation is intentional, and the abuser prepares to harm you in a psychological way.

You think that all the wrong things are happening accidentally, but the abuser knows what you feel. The extreme covert manipulators are known as psychopaths and narcissists. They follow a systematic emotional attack to break your confidence and control your realities, and you end up as their puppet without knowing that at all.

In covert manipulation, the abuser shows you a twisted reality. This misguided reality brainwashes you and ruins your ability to make correct decisions; then, the abuser guides as he or she pleases.

Overt manipulation includes all those techniques, which the victim can experience and notice, so the physical, verbal and sexual abuses come into this category. It is a situation where you have a higher tendency of knowing that you are being manipulated, but some folks may still end up not knowing what to do about it.

Both overt and covert manipulation deserve to be on your watch list that is for sure, and we will find ways to deal with them later on!

The Different Types of Manipulators

According to the manipulation techniques, you can come across the following kinds of manipulators:

1. The Expert

"I am better than you at everything."

This person wants to stay on top of every situation. These manipulators are driven by their desire to attain a strong social dominance over others. Their personalities include a high ego, which they blend with their ability to locate vulnerable people. These people like to keep people who lack self-confidence, which serves their ego.

Using insults and put-downs, these manipulators exploit the vulnerability of their victims. They are narcissistic, but hide their arrogance with fake politeness. At the core, these manipulators have self-doubts and shame. Manipulation becomes their technique to hide their own vulnerability.

2. The Perpetual Victim

"People hurt me and use me all the time."

In every scenario, you find these manipulators showcasing themselves as victims. Even if the situation has nothing to do with them, they find a way to become the victim. If you cut your fingers by mistake, this manipulator starts getting a headache and blames you for that.

By becoming a victim, these manipulators cause fights and arguments around them. You might argue with others for this person, and they stay behind the scenes and, after every argument or fight, this person will behave as a victim again. This gives power to emotionally control others and gain their sympathy at the same time.

These manipulators seek more attention from their surroundings. You can see them feeling angry and emotionally distressed. They blame their shortcomings on others' hatred for them. They use "ethics" as their manipulation card so many times and project paranoia about everything.

3. Strong Dependents

"Please follow my lead to save me from my life."

These manipulators are strong and weak at the same time. They present themselves as a powerless creature, but they are very much in control from the inside. They like to depend on someone else for their needs. In order to gain that control, they show as if they are weak and unable to live on their own. Giving compliments is the secret weapon they use to obtain control over victims.

The moment you judge them as inferior and try to help, they gain control over you. One by one, all their responsibilities become yours, and if you try to avoid them, they make you feel as if you are letting them down like how others have.

4. The Angry Beast

"How dare you ask me that, it is not my fault at all!"

These manipulators won't let you blame them for anything. They keep people away by using anger as their guard. Teenagers usually showcase these tendencies for a while;

however, they aren't aware of their behavior. On the other hand, a manipulator deliberately shows anger.

In many relationships, one partner shows anger if asked about stealing behavior, increasing credit card bills, or cheating. No matter how politely you ask, their reply is always over the top. They constantly avoid confrontation and play the blame game with their partner. For example, a manipulator can blame the partner for his/her affair saying, "I had an affair because you weren't spending enough time with me." A strong denial is their key to keep doing what they want to do so they can scream or physically abuse you if confronted strongly.

5. The Wrong Well-wisher

"I am the only friend you have in this world. Others want to eat you alive."

Lying, hiding the complete story and other manipulation techniques are valuable tools for these manipulators. They want to isolate you from family and friends by feeding lies in your mind. At the same time, they present themselves as your only well-wisher who is on your side no matter what. Alliance creation is the way they live their lives. Their friendly nature doesn't allow you to figure out their true intentions. They gradually create a strong bond with their victim, keeping their nasty intentions hidden. Then, the series of rumors begin and the manipulator becomes the source of information for the victim. They hurt emotionally with their lies and trigger hatred and anger in their victim's mind.

Friends, parents or colleagues, anyone can be this manipulator in your life. For instance, between two close girlfriends, one can start spreading rumors about another's character, just because she has a crush on her friend's boyfriend.

6. The Truth Twister

"Sorry, I think I have misinterpreted what you told me."

Using half-truths, exaggerations, and lies, these manipulators gain control over victims. They smartly alter the victim's words and turn them into reputation-harming rumors. When exposed, they simply deny and apologize by saying, "I misunderstood your words." These people want to feel superior in their group, even if they don't deserve it. Their friendly nature allows them to blend and bond with people to exploit their vulnerable sides. Gaining personal information is the first step they make, and then they create a misinterpreted story around that information. They have the capacity to justify their actions and play victim if confronted.

7. The Stubborn Deniers

"You are bad and I am good. Period."

Filled with a vast amount of ego, these manipulators deny their own behavior and actions. They usually don't understand their own flaws and project those flaws in others. For example, such a manipulator can say, "You are a racist person," even when they have racist tendencies. They see their faults and think that the world has those faults. These manipulators blame their victims and even try to include other people in their blame game. Their stubborn nature doesn't let them realize their own flaws. They actually believe that their actions and beliefs are always right.

For example, such a manipulator will point out the laziness of their victim, when he is the lazy one. In his mind, he will create justifications for his own laziness.

8. The Charming Flirt

"I am gorgeous, so give me what I want."

Attracting people and controlling them, that is how these manipulators operate. Their attractive looks become their weapon. Superficial in nature, these people feel more attractive than they actually are. They have to be the favorite person in every person's life; however, they only care about their needs and desires. Flirtatious nature and sexual triggers help these manipulators lure their victims. They want you to react to their flirtatious behavior in a positive way. These manipulators love creating tension among family members and friends.

These manipulators never stop looking for new partners. They connect with current partners strongly, but keep looking for new potential partners. They don't believe in traditional relationship structures of society. In fact, when friendships and families break, it empowers these manipulators. They want to twist people's relationships and live life like a grand drama show.

9. The Intimidator

"If I get mad, it won't be good for you!"

These manipulators get what they want by using intimidation. They bully others and demand things. They want to become the answer to "what," "why," "when" and "how" for their victims. Anything you do or say, it has to be according to their preference. These manipulators mostly use their physical features to bully others. In fact, many don't mind using physical abuse to intimidate their victims.

But the intimidation is not limited to physically strong people. Many manipulators can showcase their intelligence as an intimidating weapon. If you disagree on something, they act surprised and showcase the evidence of their superiority over you. Their belief lies in forcing their thoughts and shape situations according to themselves. For these manipulators, other people are nothing but tools, which they can use whenever desired. If they can't, their aggression is always there to make people do what they want.

10. The Adaptable Manipulator

"I observe people before I pick my manipulation tools."

These manipulators are probably the most dangerous ones. They have mastery over all the above-mentioned manipulations. They can adapt and change their behavior according to the personality of his or her victims. They combine multiple techniques together to create a perfect mix of manipulation blend that you can't escape. Even if they fail once, they don't stop. They learn and try new things to gain control over the victims. If a person resists manipulation, these manipulators feel thrilled. They search for strong personalities and carefully test their skills of manipulation.

How Manipulation is Started and its Roots

Since the beginning of human society, we have been seeking approval of others. We are asked to be nice to others and always think about the good of others. This behavior creates a certain level of vulnerability in people's personalities. A constant search for approval makes us a perfect victim for manipulators.

The roots of manipulation go deep in our nature to seek approval. The moment you give too much importance to another's point of view about your personality, your mind becomes vulnerable. You start collecting judgments about yourself and create self-hatred in your mind. These things are happening in your mind, even if you don't realize it because "seeking approval" is the basic reason why you feel stressed about everything in your life. One bad outfit choice becomes a matter of embarrassment for you. One bad picture of yours on social media scares you to death. Similarly, there are hundreds of scenarios when you overreact, when you shouldn't.

Social media platforms are a perfect example of how people are hungry for attention. Others' approval has become extremely important for us so if we don't get at least 500 hundred likes on our picture, we aren't beautiful.

When living a life of self-doubt, one day someone appears and explains how amazing you are. This person can be your lover, your boss, or your friend as well. Now, you have finally found the approval you have been looking for since your childhood so you do everything to please that person. That is how a manipulator gains power over your personality.

Reasons Why People Seek Approval from Others

There are five major reasons why people seek approval from others:

1. Low confidence and self-esteem

Low confidence is majorly the result of a bad childhood. Regular criticism from parents, teachers and other elders create a case of self-doubt in a child's mind. This child grows with low confidence and suffers from a lack of self-esteem. All those childhood criticisms become a voice in this person's mind so the person keeps attacking his own abilities in his mind.

To conquer that constant voice of self-loathing, the person seeks approval from others. Such a person seeks approval from friends, family members, a spouse and professional colleagues. To obtain that, these people easily get manipulated and do things to fulfill other people's wishes. A father-son relationship can have this equation, where the father manipulates his son to get married. This is a personal decision for an individual, but a person with low esteem can allow his father to manipulate just to seek the family's approval.

2. Low life achievements

There are two kinds of achievements that a person can gain.

One type satisfies the inner-self, while other achievements only satisfy the outer world. If a person is unhappy with his own life achievements, he or she turns towards others for approval. These people want others to tell them how great their life is. This tendency also subjects to getting manipulated.

3. Reduced personal performance

Some people work harder when their performance gets reduced; however, some people try to fill that space with false praise. People suffering from reduced performance in life like to talk about their old achievements. They tell stories to others and self-praise. Plus, they desire praise from others as well. This sends clear signs of vulnerability to manipulators.

4. No personal fulfillment

People don't feel fulfilled with what they have. They want to present themselves as bigger than they actually are. Their achievements seem low to them, but they want people to approve that they are big in terms of career, beauty, financial state and other things.

Such people seek approval to justify their ego and attain fulfillment in life. This nature makes them a victim of manipulation too many times in their lives.

5. Too much stress

Stress can also be a reason for seeking approval. When life seems out of control, people want someone else to tell them that everything is going to be fine. Even if it is true, they accept it as truth because their mind wants to get rid of the increased stress.

Most people argue that they are not vulnerable and they do not seek approval from others; however, most of us are trying to get recognized and making ourselves vulnerable in the process.

When you seek approval, manipulators come out to make you comfortable. They present themselves as a perfect solution to all your emotional and life issues. Approval seekers allow manipulators to paint an altered picture in which life has no dark colors. In return, you give your control over to that manipulator.

If you are not aware of your own emotional state, someone is going to take advantage of that. In fact, you should also listen to what others are saying and why they are saying that. Of course, manipulators do that too, but you are just trying to save yourself, instead of using others.

Understanding yourself and other people's behavior is the key to live without being manipulated. This takes us to our next chapter where you will learn how to understand your own psychology.

CHAPTER 2 – Why We Want To Know More About Ourselves

An examination of your inner-self:

Since childhood, Jennifer learned from her parents that expressing emotions is important. People love you more when they understand you better and, if a person is too rigid to express his or her emotions, it leads to loneliness.

This was the psychological conditioning that Jennifer went through all her childhood, but, as she grew up, her personality started becoming too vulnerable towards her surroundings.

Jennifer is a skilled content creator in an advertising company now, but her lack of confidence doesn't allow her to get recognition. This lack of confidence is not in her skill; instead, she shows emotional vulnerability where it is not required. She tends to apologize too much, even for small things. She worries whether people like her or not. In fact, she asks her colleagues if they like her. These behavioral traits are leading people away from her, which is completely opposite of what her parents told her.

A certain level of emotional vulnerability is good in relationships, but too much leaves you open for manipulation. Jennifer has lost many promotions to others and has faced bad relationship experiences in her 26 years of life.

Emotional vulnerability majorly comes from our psychological conditioning from childhood; however, some current scenarios can also trigger emotional vulnerability from time to time. It is your responsibility to notice that state.

Signs That Say You Are Emotionally Vulnerable

1. You fall in love too easily

Someone smiles at your joke and you create a love story in your mind. Some stranger opens a door for you and you begin your journey of love with that person. Simple acts of kindness and general affection makes you fall in love with a person.

You might be thinking that it is too much, "I don't fall in love so easily," but think about all those times when simple things made you fall for a person.

Love is a connection you feel after a long period of emotional bonding; however, emotionally, vulnerable people get triggered by simple acts. If this happens to you too often, then you should sit and think about your emotional state.

Such vulnerability usually occurs when you have just gone through a rough break-up. Your heart looks for a rebound to revive its state of happiness; however, a wrong partner selection does nothing but hurt you more. You can find a stranger attractive in a single glance, but don't let your heart get emotionally attached without a strong bonding.

2. You don't have any emotional shareholder

Think of your mind as a company, and emotions as shares of that company. If you give that share to everyone, it reduces the strength of your company but, at the same time, handling all those shares alone can become difficult.

When emotions stay collected in your mind and you don't share them, it creates emotional vulnerability. Your problems become the driving force in your life as they guide you. With that comes the need for social approval from everyone.

If you don't share your problems with anyone, that would be a red alert sign. You aren't opening up, even when others share their problems. Of course, you need to stay away from manipulators, but find at least one person who is genuine and ready to listen. Even talking about your problems with the right person can resolve the issue, but make sure you choose a genuine person to share with and not a manipulator.

3. You do everything to hold people in your life

Even if others treat you bad, you want them to stay around you. For that, you do everything that they ask and everything that you might think they would like. This process exhausts you emotionally, but still, you don't find the strength to let people go.

Every relationship in your life is worth the fight if it is a good relationship, but when you allow people to treat you bad and use you in every possible way it shows your emotional vulnerability. This emotional state is not usually in your control. You stay aware that the other person doesn't deserve your attention, but you feel helpless.

4. You're always the first one to say "sorry"

If 10 people make a mistake, you come out first to apologize, even when you are not one of those ten people. You apologize after every third statement and feel sorry for very small things.

Low self-esteem and self-doubt meet an approval-seeking behavior in this kind of vulnerability. You don't feel that you deserve anything, and you apologize to stay on the good books of people around you. Even a stranger's point of view matters to you. If a stranger's bike hits your car, you come out to apologize first without even expecting an apology from the other person.

5. You're suspicious that people don't like you

Self-doubt can make you doubt other people's affection towards you. You start questioning the affection of a friend who has been with you since childhood. You not only think like this, but also vocalize your thoughts many times.

In your office, family gatherings and normal meetings, you keep throwing a question around, "I don't know if he/she really likes me." This gives a chance to a manipulator to confirm your suspicions and become your sole friend.

Liking yourself is the most important affection you need. If you feel satisfied with your inner-self, other people will like you automatically. In fact, seeking approval can create issues in your relationships. People who actually like you might feel offended because you question their affection again and again.

Just do good, be good, and forget about whether people like you or not!

6. Every relationship break gives you the same amount of pain

Whether a crush doesn't reply to your text, or your partner cheats on you, both are the same in terms of pain for you. No matter how strong or new a relationship is, you feel crushed when someone hurts. Even if a professional colleague doesn't return your call, you feel disrespected and denied.

These extreme emotions make you vulnerable. Any manipulator can satisfy your emotions and get control over your personality. A manipulator can feed lies and easily make you isolated from other relationships.

7. Loved ones decide how you feel today

Your moods are not in your control. You feel happy only if your loved ones feel happy. If they feel sad, your mood becomes gloomy for the whole day. Of course, it shows your love for people around you, but the sudden switch of mood also means that you are vulnerable and easily manipulated by other people's emotions. If a manipulator enters your life as a partner, a boss or a loved one, you will easily give away your emotional control to them.

8. You cry alone

The whole day goes fine, you go out with your friends, have fun, smile, laugh, and come back home, and then a glass falls and you start crying. A sad song has the capacity to switch your happy mood to a gloomy emotion, and then you cry as if the world has fallen apart.

This state of mind is extremely critical because you aren't aware of this vulnerability. You live as two personalities, and the sorrowful personality comes out only when you are alone, and it is so intense that you have no control over it so you start looking for someone who can control your heart for you. That is what leads to manipulation in some cases. If you are lucky, you get an angel or a prince charming with a bright heart. If not so lucky, you end up giving your emotional control to a devil in disguise.

There is no shame in accepting your vulnerability. In fact, it empowers you as a person and allows you to become a better version of yourself. You don't just think extremely about "love and hate." Your mind finds a grey area where some people and relationships can exist. You trust yourself and love your own personality. Other people's judgments become a second priority. This is the first step towards diminishing your approval- seeking behavior.

Difference between being "Nice" and being "Manipulated"

Aren't we always advised to be nice to others? Should we stop being nice if people are out there to manipulate our niceness?

NO. That's not right; however, there is a difference between being nice and being manipulated.

Some people CHOOSE to be nice, while others are nice inherently. A person who chooses to be nice has control over his or her niceness. He or she can be nice to the genuine people only and save themselves from being manipulated.

On the other hand, people, who are inherently nice, become vulnerable in front of a manipulator. They don't have control over their nice behavior, which leads to manipulation many times. Just because you don't say no to work, you get more work than other people in your office. The boss is always on your head with unimaginable deadlines.

It all leads back to the conditioning that you gained from your parents and school. Our teachers and parents forget to tell us about the "choice of being nice," and that skipped chapter creates vulnerability in our lives.

Let's consider a scenario:

One day, Victor went shopping for groceries from the supermarket. There was a long line in front of the checkout. Victor was behind three people and a little girl was behind him.

When Victor reached the counter, he allowed the little girl to buy her candies before him. The girl bought and left but, just after that, a woman, with three children, crosses Victor saying, "I am in a hurry, please."

Now, Victor has two choices. He can allow that lady to cut him and buy her items first, or stop her.

If Victor is inherently nice, he would let the lady buy first, but that would allow others to cut him in the line too. However, if Victor is someone who chooses to be nice, he will notice that this lady has seen him as a potential victim because of the earlier scenario with the little girl.

We all come across thousands of scenarios like this when our visible niceness makes us a potential victim for manipulators. You can choose not to allow those people to use your niceness to their advantage.

Reasons Why "Being Too Nice" is a Wrong Choice

1. You come across as a weak personality

"Oh! You're a nice guy, you won't say no." People assume that you would do everything they ask in advance. This is the biggest hazard of being too nice to others. Whenever there is a problem, people burden you with that problem without even asking whether you need that problem or not. Your responsibilities are yours, and others' responsibilities are yours as well.

You say "yes" to help a person twice, and he will hand over the responsibility the third time with complete confidence that you are available at his or her service. People stop caring about your personal responsibilities, your time, and even your emotional state. They think you are weak because you never say no to anyone, and that leads to manipulation and exploitation of your niceness.

2. Some wrong people get attracted to you

Be too nice and get ready for "not so nice" people in your life. This is the harsh reality of real life. Even people, who hide their whiny, angry and bad sides, force all those emotions towards a nice person. In a way, your niceness allows the bad side of others to come out and attack you.

People, who are too nice, find themselves around manipulators very often. People start demanding things from you, instead of requesting. They control your moves and shift your actions as they please. This happens anywhere you go. Unlike manipulation, niceness becomes visible easily. Your family, your partner, your colleagues and even strangers give you a hard time.

3. You forget to appreciate yourself

You have an appointment with your doctor, but your boss

wants you to manage a meeting for him.

Or, you want to relax this weekend, but your friend has asked you to fix his bike.

Others become a priority when you are too nice. You don't know how to say no because he is your boss, or she is your friend. But guess what? You have been with yourself since the day you were born, but nice people forget that and give their life to others.

Forgetting yourself in an act of niceness makes you a perfect victim of manipulation. People think of you whenever they need something, and forget the moment you do that thing for them. This leaves you hurt, but mostly your niceness doesn't allow you to learn anything from bad experiences.

4. People stop taking you seriously

When you say nothing but "yes" to everything, your point of view becomes useless to others. You are never disappointed at anything, so your children or colleagues don't ask for your opinion on anything. You never push back; hence, your own projects are completed with your juniors' inputs. You lose your perspective on things, or at least don't find the right way to express those perspectives.

There is no nice way to say that something is wrong; hence, people with too much niceness fail to create an impact on their surroundings, whether it is their household or workspace.

5. People think you are fake

Too much niceness makes your personality suspicious to others. People think that you are faking and your real side is not so nice. This creates a sense of distrust, which leads people away. That is why nice people don't get promotions or find a leading spot in projects. People in your life stop trusting you with important information. They think you are going to use them in some way, while you are the one being manipulated constantly.

Manipulators around you can trigger rumors about your niceness. They can turn your niceness into an evil thing and take advantage of that. As people feel strangely about your niceness, convincing them is never difficult that you are faking it all.

6. You are unable to give tough love

People who are too nice never thrive in a leading position. As a father, a team leader or a boss, such people feel unable to perform.

You can't be nice to your people all the time. Sometimes, they need tough love to grow and become better, but a nice person doesn't know how to project that tough love. Pushing your staff to complete a project, or asking your kid to work harder on his skills, requires a little roughness. It should be a perfect balance of niceness, logic and toughness that motivates people. Without this combination, you can't act as a leader.

Saying, "Please, sit down son, it might make you angry" won't work at all. Your son would know that you expect him to get angry when you talk. Also, you can't talk in circles and try to find a nice way to say the honest thing. Sometimes, ripping off the bandage is the right way to make others realize that you exist. Even if the ripping might take off a little skin with it.

Why Do Nice People Feel Angry So Often?

The thought behind being nice is that you receive happiness in return, but that happiness doesn't come to you very often. If you are nice enough to let manipulators control you, it results in anger and regret.

Nice people feel happy during an act of kindness but then they realize that they were being manipulated. The end feeling is anger towards the manipulator, as well as oneself. This only happens when your niceness is blinded by the tactics of manipulators.

Your goal should be to be nice without falling into the trap of a manipulator. Only then, you can stay happy and avoid anger.

Manipulators love when they see certain traits in a person. They carefully choose their targets who are vulnerable and too nice.

Everyone has doubts, fears, wishes, gratitude, hopes, love and other feelings, but the vulnerable personalities are the ones that don't know about their own emotional and psychological conditions. Manipulators observe that and try to manipulate their victims.

You don't have to become an unsympathetic or senseless person to avoid manipulation; simply understand your inner-self before a manipulator does.

Here are 10 traits that manipulators love to exploit:

1. Fear of "looking like a loser"

If you have a strong fear of looking like a loser, manipulators would love to exploit this fear sometimes for an advantage, but many times just for fun. Manipulators love to play with insecurity in order to satisfy their own ego. They want to feel powerful and find exploitation exciting. Remember all those situations when your friends provoked you to do something you didn't want to do. You face such manipulators in school, college and at a professional level as well. Even some family members can exploit your fear and insecurities to have fun.

Whenever you feel scared of looking like a loser, stop and think. First of all, think about whether you actually want to do that thing or not. If yes, then think about whether you want to do it right there and then. We all give ourselves some adventurous tasks in life, but everything has a right place and a right time. You shouldn't just have your first drink because your friends are provoking you. Even if you want to do it, decide a safe time and choose a safe environment to do it. Never take a risk just because someone else wants you to. Confidently say no, and tell them when you would do that thing. Expect them to understand if they are friends as manipulators are there to just provoke you.

2. Feeling of guilt

Guilt is probably the most favorite trait that a manipulator wants to see in a target. If you are suffering from guilt, you tend to do every possible thing to get rid of that feeling. Manipulators impose guilt on their vulnerable targets to play with their emotions. Once you accept that you are guilty of something, they use that guilt to make you do things for them.

This happens even when you haven't done anything wrong. You see, some people have a tendency to feel guilty about everything. They are ready to apologize for everything, as mentioned earlier. This trait attracts and draws a manipulator toward you.

When feeling guilty, question your guilt before acting. Are you guilty enough to feel that bad? Even if it is true, you can apologize with all your heart, but don't follow instructions of another person who might be controlling your guilt. If a person points out why you should be feeling guiltier, he or she is not there to help you. Manipulators highlight the extreme consequences of your actions and constantly tell you to feel guilty. You can't predict another's emotional reaction to your actions. You can just try to be as good as possible so don't be too hard on yourself and stay away from people who impose guilt on you for no reason.

3. Fear of "rejection"

When you hear your parents say, "I will love you as long as you get good grades," it creates a fear of rejection in your mind. You grow up with that same feeling and feel the pressure of performing every single second to gain acceptance from people around you. A teacher, a friend or others around us can induce the feeling of rejection in us, and then manipulators appear in the form of a partner, a boss or a friend to exploit this fear. A manipulative lover can ask a lot of things in return for staying in a relationship with you. This exploitation can be related to money, emotions or other elements.

You are not on this planet to provide your endless service to others. Your life is your first priority and I am not saying that in a selfish way and others come after that. You need to fulfill yourself on an emotional level before giving something to others, and if people around you are trying to gain something in return of their affection, they don't deserve you. An emotional attachment has to be selfless and mutual. It is not a business exchange and, if it is, then you have to get out of those relationships. Love needs nothing but love in return, so don't let anyone make you feel rejected, because no one can.

4. Sense of responsibility

We all have some responsibilities in our lives. Most people understand their responsibilities and fulfill them casually; however, there are people who are driven by their sense of being responsible. They feel a duty towards their family, friends, company, society, roads, shops, dogs and so on. Everything is their responsibility to fulfill. A manipulator sees such people as an opportunity. Close relatives, friends, and colleagues use such people to get what they want. Such people are the most vulnerable to manipulation. Anyone can play the "duty card" and manipulate such people successfully.

Completing your duties are important, but those duties should be yours. If others are creating duties and putting a burden on your shoulder, you need to evaluate your behavior. Turning down your close friend or boss can seem difficult; so you need to ensure that you don't go overboard and harm yourself in the process. Find a balance and prioritize which responsibilities are necessary. Don't just say yes to a transfer because your boss wants you to do so. Think about your personal growth and future plans first. Similarly, it is not your responsibility to pay for your partner's expensive shopping lists. Find a middle ground of responsibilities.

5. Pity and kindness

Do you have compassion and kindness? Some manipulative fellows are out there to use your emotions to their advantage. These manipulators exaggerate their situations to gain your attention. Usually, their conditions are as normal as others, but they ensure that you look at them with pity. These fellows are in your family and in your friend circle as well. You can even find such people in your office. The moment you show pity towards them, they don't miss to ask for what they need from you, and you end up helping someone who doesn't require your compassion.

You need to learn to control your kindness as well. Use kind words instead of helping a manipulator. If you sense that the person is trying to impose something on you, reply with a compliment, "You are talented enough to come out of this crisis." This way, you will stop manipulators from exploiting your kindness.

6. Gratitude

A manipulator plans strategically to use your gratitude for their benefit. A manipulative friend will help you with 500 bucks and ask for 10,000 bucks as help. If you say, "I am short on money these days," he would remind you about the 500 bucks he gave you without even thinking twice. You can't say that it was only 500 bucks. To that, he would question your friendship. Some manipulators consciously create such complicated environments to ask for a big help by reminding you about their small act of kindness. Also, there are people who do this without knowing.

If there wasn't a previous contract, you are not obliged to

return the favor. You can help as much as convenient for you, but don't react to the unfair manipulation and let someone use you because of their old favor. Politely counter people who remind you about their favors and explain that you are ready to offer as much help as convenient.

7. Shame

People feel ashamed when their actions don't match the fundamentals of life and society. If publically exploited, the feeling of shame is easily manipulated. For instance, if you question before donating money to a charity, the manipulators can induce the feeling of shame by saying, "You should feel ashamed of your heartlessness." Any person would try to avoid this feeling; hence, you end up being manipulated and used in the process of saving yourself from shameful feelings.

When you make a mistake, it induces the feeling of shame. You can apologize for that and move on, but the wrong situation occurs when someone is constantly trying to induce shame in you. If some other person has certain expectations that you can't meet, it is not shameful at all. If you let it affect you, manipulators will get complete control over your actions. This can lead to some bad scenarios that leave you angry and regretful.

8. Feeling of loneliness

Humans require socialization, but one should also find contentment when they are alone as well. Some people constantly fear that they will end up alone. This feeling attracts manipulators in your life. They know you would do everything for them to keep them so they start by creating a strong bond and finding an important place in your life. Then, the manipulation begins. It is common between a husband and wife, where one partner says, "No one would want you if I leave you." This statement is a constant reminder that a manipulator gives you so that you stay afraid of loneliness.

To avoid such situations, you have to have faith in yourself. Love yourself before loving others and give respect to your own personality. If you can successfully do that, no manipulator would dare scare you.

9. Excessive vanity

Some people are easily pleased, which harms them in many phases of life. A manipulator throws a compliment and catches you in the trap of working for him or her. Your boss can say, "You're the best employee I have, so do this task by tomorrow." People with excessive vanity get manipulated with such requests and end up being used constantly.

Flattery compliments can be a disguise so you need to evaluate the person who is complimenting you. Think about the reasons he or she could be giving you compliments. Control your inner ego and stop looking for validation for your performance, work or skills. When you are confident enough about your abilities, no compliment actually flatters you too much. This way, you can think logically and avoid manipulation.

10. Hope

Manipulators let you see altered futures with all your hopes fulfilled. They keep feeding you lies in order to gain benefits at present. They say that the result of today's work will become visible in future. A boyfriend can ask you to marry him and promise a great life ahead, even if he is not working currently. Similarly, a boss can manipulate you to work overtime today so that you can get a promotion at the end of the project.

Your hope should not come in the way of logical reasoning. You need to assess others' intentions before falling for their promises.

You definitely experience all the above-mentioned emotions from time to time. The goal is to understand your emotions and the intentions of the manipulators in order to save yourself.

Manipulation does not have to be part of your life, or at the very least it should be brought down to the barest minimum such that it does not rear its ugly mug wherever you go. At this juncture, I would like to sincerely ask that if you have found some or even just one piece of value from all of the above, would you be so kind as to leave a review over at amazon and share with folks on what you have liked and taken away so far, that would mean a great deal and be really awesome. Note: no manipulation here!

CHAPTER 3 – Doing This One Thing Can Literally Save Your Life!

Travelers, writers, and artists talk intellectually about life and people. How do they do that?

A person who spends a lot of time in isolation becomes self-aware, and that self-awareness allows that person to understand how other people think, behave and react.

However, you don't have to isolate yourself in order to become self-aware. Taking correct steps in your daily life can allow you to explore your inner-self conveniently.

Why Do You Need To Become Self-Aware?

Forget about manipulators for a while, self-awareness is meaningful no matter whether you have manipulators in your life or not. A comprehensive understanding of your own personality helps you point out your weaknesses and strengths. You keep stirring your thoughts and emotions and modify your beliefs in the process.

In life, all our actions are motivated by our inner personality and beliefs. Knowing the reasons behind every action can allow you to assess before making any decision. That is what leads to success and personal contentment in life.

Self-awareness also makes you capable of learning other

people's perceptions. You can detect the reasons behind their actions and words and decide your actions carefully. It all can seem like a formula, but, with practice, it becomes your lifestyle. Knowing others' perception is not like what manipulators do. You are not trying to use people's emotions to your advantage. In fact, you are able to assess others' emotions and try to help them with no bad intentions. That is the difference between a manipulator and a self-aware person.

The irony is that everyone thinks they have achieved self-awareness completely. If you ask any person, he or she will accept that they know their behavior completely, but self-awareness is not just about knowing your behavior. It is about knowing why you are behaving that way and what beliefs are motivating you to behave that way. A self-aware person knows his or her wrong beliefs and tries to diminish them in a gradual process. A self-aware person knows which emotions are harming his or her life. That is how one can begin to change and find one's best version.

The process of developing self-awareness helps you understand new and better interpretations of personal thoughts. You find out that your mental state was creating your thoughts and developing emotions. You develop enhanced emotional intelligence and stop allowing emotions to control your actions. This control over emotions saves you from handing over the control to a manipulator; however, it is important to remember that self-awareness is a gradual process. You can't think that one day of practice is enough to achieve mastery over your emotions. You have to pick emotions one-by-one and understand how strongly they define your personality. Some people are driven by love, while the sense of responsibility motivates others. All these factors require an in-depth assessment.

Every emotion, thought or behavior leads to a pre-decided path. You have to know which emotions or thoughts will lead you in a wrong direction. For instance, if you know that your sense of gratitude will make you vulnerable to manipulation, you can work to save yourself from the false flattery.

You can become immune to manipulation only by knowing your inner-self. The person living inside you requires a master. Either you can become that master, or a manipulator will appear in your life to take that place. Self-awareness is the course that you need to master your inner-self. Plus, you can focus your mental and emotional energy towards things that lead to a better future. You start reacting to things that actually matter, instead of getting affected by everything and everyone around you.

And finally, all your efforts help you love and believe in yourself. You know that you can win anything in your life just by focusing your inner energy towards it. This improves self-confidence and self-respect in a person, which is exactly what you need to avoid manipulation.

Top 10 Ways to Increase Self-Awareness

First of all, you should accept that there is no one-time formula to become self-aware. You can't take one pill and become aware of all your emotions, thoughts and motivations. It is a continuous exercise. The more vulnerable you are, the deeper you have to dig in order to find issues and resolve. People, who are vulnerable emotionally, usually hide some dark experiences deep in their mind. The way you were raised and the experiences you have received until now, all decide the work you need to do in order to become self-aware.

If you do it regularly, a self-aware lifestyle becomes automatic.

Here are 10 valuable steps that will help you exercise and make self-awareness your lifestyle:

1. Evaluate your motivations

Our motivations allow us to set our goals and work towards it to achieve that goal; however, you don't reach every goal that you feel motivated about.

It is time that you understand your motivations and how they drive your life. First, in a diary, write down two goals that you decided and achieved in the past. These goals should be dearest to you. Only then, you would become able to evaluate them properly. For each goal achieved, ask the following questions to yourself:

1. Why did you want to achieve that goal?

2. Which reasons helped you reach that goal?

3. How easy or difficult was the work for you to reach that goal?

4. Why do you still remember that goal?

Write down answers to these questions for both the goals you have achieved in your life. After that, you can move to two goals that you HAVEN'T REACHED yet and feel disappointed about. For each failure, ask the following questions to yourself:

1. Why did you choose that goal?

2. What reasons were out of your control that stopped you from achieving that goal?

3. Were there some things you could do to control the situations better?

4. How easy or difficult was the work when you were trying?

5. What are the things you missed in life, giving your time to that goal?

6. Why do you feel disappointed and how much?

After answering these questions, you can compare your achievements and failures. Try to find similarities in your motivations, and also, look at the differences between motivations. This way, you will know why you won sometimes and failed in a few things in your life.

Remember, these goals are not limited to career or education. You can include monetary, fitness, personal, love and other life goals and evaluate your motivations. This evaluation will help you understand why a relationship didn't work and your mistakes that led to the destruction of a relationship.

2. Become the only friend you need

It is good to have friends in life. A beautiful friendship nourishes our mental state and allows us to grow as a person, but you can't keep waiting for a genuine friend to appear one day and sort all your emotional problems. Instead, you should become your own friend and attain a bonding with your inner-self.

To do that, you need to start by noticing how much time you spend with yourself. Spending time with yourself means that you sit alone and stir your thoughts and have a conversation in your own head. It might seem a little crazy, but thought-stirring is an important task to understand your mind.

Make a list of independent decisions. In life, you make thousands of decisions including the big ones and the small ones, and most people get affected by others' thought process while making decisions. Of course, people's suggestions help us choose the right things in life, but if all your decisions are based on what others say, then it is a bad sign. There should be a few decisions that you make on your own.

To test yourself, you should make a list including all those decisions that you have made independently. If you want to start small, list all the small or big decisions you have made this week on your own.

If the number of independent decisions is low, then you need to work towards it and become more self-dependent.

Make a list of things you do alone: Listening to music, exercise, reading, writing, or any other activity; doing things alone is not about physical loneliness. You should be able to do things and enjoy them even if no other person is taking part in it. In fact, you should deliberately create such scenarios in order to spend time with your inner-self. Making this list will allow you to know how independent you are. If you only go out if your friends say yes, then you need to make some changes. Why not go out for a walk or a long drive alone? These activities will get you closer to your inner-self.

Give yourself 30 minutes every day: Give at least 15 minutes when no thought from the outer world can enter your mind. Don't even listen to music, those are also outer thoughts. You need things that allow you to manufacturer and stir thoughts in your mind. You can go for a nature walk near your place, meditate, or do something creative alone. Every day, you hear millions of things and it all keeps you outside of your mind but, when you are alone, outer thoughts start fading away slowly and you meet the true thoughts of your inner-self. That is what you need to achieve every day.

3. Write problems your inner-self has with the outer world

All your problems in life begin when your inner-self is not in sync with the outer world. You can also say that your surrounding can bury your inner-self, while you pretend on the outside to be a happy person. It is important to find and evaluate those problems.

When you said "yes," instead of "no": In our everyday life, we tend to say "yes" to people, even when we desire to say "no." This is how the problems begin. Your inner-self knows when you should say "no," but your sense of fear, responsibility, affection, pity and other things don't allow you that so you end up doing things that you really don't want to do. Now, you need to make a list of such situations and audit your problems. Start with the previous week and write all the situations when you said "yes." See if you really wanted to say that or if it was imposed on you. Also, figure out which emotions led you to say "yes" forcefully.

Outer elements that you don't like: There are places, media, activities, and people in everyone's life. Some elements excite us and offer pleasure, while others make us feel negative, exhausted or bored. Make a list of all those elements and start eliminating them from your life one-by-one.

Elimination of negative elements is not about going away from them. If you can, it's awesome! However, you can't go away from a negative office environment or leave a close person in your life. The idea of elimination is to not allow those people, activities or places to harm your inner-self. You can stop indulging your mind in the conversations you don't like. Make those elements a formality in your life without letting them impact you emotionally.

Set some boundaries: Decide a limit for all the negative things that you can handle. A boundary is a comfortable limit to which your inner-self can manage negative things without feeling disturbed. If your outer world crosses that boundary, immediate elimination is the only choice.

4. Talk to your emotions

In the realm of emotions, words are not the communication model, but your emotions talk to you. It is your own cognitive awareness that decides how well you understand them.

Differentiating emotions: The first step towards talking to your emotions is to identify them. This might seem easy when you are differentiating emotions such as "happiness" and "sadness." However, it becomes difficult for people to differentiate whether they are feeling "sad" or "overwhelmed."

Studies suggest that naming your emotions can help in understanding them so, instead of saying "I am scared," you can say "Mr. Scary has entered my brain." This would allow you to see emotions as a third-person and manage them effectively.

Understanding the language of your emotions: Every emotion tries to send a message. It is your self-awareness that allows you to decipher that message correctly.

So, what does sadness say to you?

Is it, "You are feeling the loss of something?"

Or, "This is what's extremely important to you!"

Similarly, what does fear tell you?

"You are a scaredy cat."

Or, "You need to concentrate while doing this."

Becoming an observer is what you need in order to talk to your emotions. Observe how emotions affect your body. Do you get all sweaty when afraid?! How does your heartbeat change with emotions? Observing the impact of emotions will allow you to dictate them.

5. Pay close attention to FEAR

Fear stops you from feeling positive, and any action caused due to fear never ends up right; however, "fear" as an emotion is not negative. It actually tells you to focus and concentrate when working, but people who aren't self-aware, misinterpret and lose control due to fear.

The emotion "fear" includes every thought that comes to your mind due to outer scenarios. Sometimes, fear is imposed by others as well so it is your responsibility to not let your inner-voice get corrupted.

To do so, you need to understand the pattern of fear. Every individual reacts with a sense of fear towards different things. Someone can feel afraid to argue with his or her partner due to the "fear of rejection." Another person can do everything asked due to the "fear of shame."

You can understand your fear better by answering these questions:

- What negative thoughts come to your mind every day?

- Which situations do you hate the most and want to avoid in your everyday life?

- What activities, things, places or people help you calm down?

These questions will allow you to understand the elements that trigger fear in your life. You will also understand the elements that help you remove that sense of fear. With that, you can try cultivating similar habits and qualities in yourself to calm yourself down on your own.

Practice affirmations: In this case, affirmations are the sentences that you say out loud to fight your fears.

For example:

If you feel afraid of something that hasn't happened yet: "I live in the NOW; the time is 'Right NOW'."

If you are afraid or worried of the result despite of your hard work:

"Practice today and enjoy success tomorrow. Success is inevitable because I am working in the present."

Similarly, you can create your own affirmations to make fear a motivational emotion. You can't get rid of fear, but these things will make fear a positive emotion.

6. Find a pattern in your behavior

You might not realize it, but your inner-self is following a pattern of behavior. Things that you learned as a child and the experiences you received growing up are still directing your present activities, perceptions and thoughts.

However, the human brain has the ability to evolve. The genetics aren't everything. Your brain uses new experiences to change your behavior regularly, but those evolutions have a certain limit depending on your core conditioning. If you can understand your behavioral patterns, it will give you the control over your thought and perception evolution.

To do that:

List your childhood lessons: Your parents, teachers and friends teach you a lot about life, relationships, work, ethics and success. Some teachings become our core ideas that drive us the whole life. You need to write all those lessons from your childhood, which you still remember. It doesn't matter whether you still follow them or not. Just include every lesson that you learned as a child.

Separate lessons that helped you: In a new list, you can include all those childhood lessons that you still follow. For instance, you still think that success is defined by a person's inner satisfaction and his ability to protect his or her loved ones. Similarly, you will find many other lessons from childhood that still influence you in a positive way and allow you to shape your present and future.

Separate lessons didn't help you: Make another list with all the childhood lessons that didn't help you at all. They were memorable growing up, but you constantly encountered contradictory situations in life. For example, your mother told you to be nice to let other people be nice to you; however, bullies were still bullying you in school. You followed the teaching of niceness as a grown-up, but people kept using you to gain advantage. These are the lessons you need to work on. You have to refine your core conditioning according to the scenarios and people you encounter in your life.

It is difficult as a parent to teach every variation of every lesson to a child. The same problem was faced by your parents when you were a kid; hence, it is time that you modify your childhood lessons and prepare yourself for the world you live in.

7. Make time your personal asset

You can't become self-aware if you don't own your time. Some people run their own time, while others run with time.

When you start owning your time, you automatically realize that most of the activities in you are worth nothing. You have been doing things just to please others. You can keep doing it, but knowing would make you self-aware, for example, whether you are going out for a dinner because YOU WANT to, or it is just one of the activities that you are obliged to fulfill as a social animal. Noticing these things will allow you to balance how much you want to indulge your inner-self for that particular time period.

Find that HIGH time of the day: Every person feels at his or her peak of mental awareness once during a day. Some people feel self-aware in the morning, while others find their inner-self at night. You need to decide that time for yourself. Actually, you need to find that time for yourself, and then make sure that you choose something that you actually want to do during this time. If you like meditation, choose your HIGH time to do it. This way, you will gain the ownership of your time.

Balance your emotional involvement: Make a list of activities you regularly indulge in without actually wanting to, and then make a habit of controlling your emotional involvement during these times. This way, your inner-self will stay protected from the negative elements of the outer world.

8. Observe your mood swings

Mood swings are a cycle of emotions created by the storage of emotions you already have in mind. Even if you go into isolation, you will still experience rage, sorrow, pain, happiness, frustration and so on. These emotions feel random at a single glance, but they all are triggered by each other. For instance, you can feel happy while thinking about an old relationship, which leads to nostalgia, and then, nostalgia can lead to the sadness of not having that person in your life now.

When you live and interact in society, these mood swings occur frequently. You can feel sad for a few hours and become happy just because your crush said "hello" to you, or your boss praised you for the work you did.

The idea of self-awareness is to observe these changes. This way, you can handle negative moods such as frustration, being overwhelmed or sadness.

Whenever you experience a strong emotion, try connecting the dots. Observe elements and thoughts that have led to the current emotional state you are in. Regular practice will create an autopilot in your mind and you will know why you are feeling a certain way within seconds.

9. Recognize stimuli for recurring emotions

Some patterns of life keep bothering you emotionally which means that you react to the similar things in the same way. They happen again and again. For instance, you can fight on the same topic with your partner and feel a combination of emotions such as sadness, anger, gloominess, and fear.

There is a way you can control these situations better:

When....(stimulus)..........happens, I feel.......(emotions)......

In the place of "stimulus" and "emotions," you can fill the triggers and the reactions you feel. This practice is for negative things that happen regularly and you react the same way.

For example, you can write:

"When my partner laughs at me, I feel angry."

This activity will help you recognize your behavior that wasn't visible to you earlier.

10. Cultivate openness of thoughts

There are two kinds of thought exchanges you indulge in life.

The first exchange is when you pass your own thought to someone else. Passing a judgment such as, "How useless you are?" or, "What is wrong with you?" The thought from your mind reaches others. Now, such thought transfer doesn't just affect the receiver, you also get a thrill of superiority in your mind. A false sense of pride comes in your mind, which stops you from finding your inner-self.

The second type of exchange is when you receive other people's thoughts. Thoughts coming from the outside can make you feel offended, hurt, angry, happy, sad, bitter, jealous, and many other things. This second type also breaks the connection between you and your inner-self. That is how a manipulator gets a hold of your actions.

So, the idea is to cultivate a sense of openness in your thoughts. Don't let negative things hurt you too much, or allow good thoughts to take you on top of the moon. Try to stay as grounded as possible. Some folks achieve that through the daily practice of meditation. It helps to clear the mind, and give stunning clarity to your own thoughts and emotions.

How to Become Socially Aware

When you are self-aware, your social awareness improves automatically; however, you can still apply a few habits to enhance your social awareness:

1. Convey that you're listening

Do you really listen to people or just pretend to be listening? Good listeners actually hear and understand how the other person is feeling; however, you should also convey that you are listening. Sending an indirect proof of your interest in the conversation can enhance your social popularity.

How can you do that?

Repeat the person's statement before replying. You don't have to repeat every sentence that the other person says. Use this once or twice in a conversation to convey your interest in the conversation.

2. Evaluate the voice tone in an ongoing conversation

People can say the same sentence with many different emotions. One can say, "You are the best employee." However, the thought behind this can only be visible by the voice tone of that person. The statement can have a sense of pride or happiness, or it can have sarcasm in it. The same words can mean different things depending on the tone of the person's voice so focus on the tone before you believe someone.

3. Understand minor facial expressions

Facial expressions and body postures send indirect cues about the person's intentions. Even if the person is trying to control his or her voice tone, the facial expressions give it away. You just need to pay attention to those cues.

For example, if you ask your partner to discuss something, and he or she replies, "Yes dear, I am here to talk," but he or she hasn't looked at you and not even moved towards you, this says that your partner is not actually interested in listening to you.

Social awareness is a combination of social sensitivity, social communication, and social insight. With practice, you cultivate the skill to comprehend social situations at a fast pace. This helps in gathering social insights and using those insights when communicating with people. The same awareness allows you to detect when a manipulator tries to overpower you with his or her tactics.

Now you have all the tools to become emotionally and socially intelligent. Make sure you practice them with determination until they become a part of your personality.

CHAPTER 4 - Workplace Manipulation And What You Can Do About It

You imagine a perfect office where people come singing happy songs and work together. Good guys spread their goodness with bright clothes on their body and a big smile on their face. Even the bad fellows of the office are visible due to their scary clothing and devil-like make-up.

Well, in a real-world office, nothing of this sort happens. You can act like a hero coming out of a Disney movie, but your co-workers won't act as open as you thought. There aren't any visible signs to acknowledge the bad guys in a real office.

You get welcomed with lots of smiles. Some of those smiling faces become your friends. You chat with them, they listen to you, in fact, "They get you." Your jokes are funny to them and you share your personal and professional insecurities with those people. However, you may find out in future that they were the ones digging holes in your way.

These people are dangerous in your professional life because they don't just do things for an ultimate goal. It is what they love. Ruining your life in the office gives them pleasure. At every step, you will find these people manipulate the scenarios and turn the spotlight of success towards themselves. They are not afraid to take risks and try everything to control your emotions and actions. If you surround yourself with such co-workers, they can even make you feel worthless.

So, if these manipulators are in every real-world office, how can we save ourselves from them? Is it inevitable for us to get into the trap of a sociopath and lose our dignity, self-esteem, and righteousness?

Let's try to find out how workplace manipulation works, and which techniques are used frequently:

Types of Workplace Manipulation

1. Boosting hope and confidence

"I have never seen such a smart professional like you. I will MAKE YOU the best employee here."

This is the very first manipulation that you go through when joining an office. Your team leader, your boss and other seniors try to include you in their groups. They want you to look up to them, so they can exploit your abilities to their advantage. You do a simple task like searching something on the internet and you are showered with compliments as if you are the Mark Zuckerberg of that office.

After the confidence boosting compliments, you receive messages from some godfathers of that office. Your talent is a tool for them to build their own career so they give you hope of becoming better if you work under them and listen to what they say. Actually, these people either don't have enough talent or procrastinate too much, so their goal is always to use you to complete their own work.

When Sam joined his first PR company, his first day at the office went like this:

Team leader: "Well, Sam, I think you have the potential to go big here. This company has the scope of growth which is perfect for a qualified person like you."

Sam: "I hope so sir! I am looking forward to not just work, but learn from my work as well. Becoming better is my ultimate goal."

Team leader: "If that's your goal, you have found the right person. I am a hard taskmaster, but I promise you, if you work hard and do as I say, you will learn a lot."

Sam: "I am ready for any task you give me sir! I am all yours."

And, for the next 6 months, Sam worked on his team leader's projects. All this time, the team leader used to come to the office late and leave early. Even in the office, the team leader spent time gossiping and fooling around. The project got completed on time though as Sam was working hard and using his skills, but all the appreciation went to the team leader because Sam was new and not involved in the "office politics."

2. Flaw projection

"These mistakes have never been made in the history of mankind. How could you do such a thing?"

Manipulators hide their unproductivity or inefficiencies with flaw projection. They shift the blame somehow towards you so that their flaws stay hidden.

"This project is ruined because I believed in you and gave you complete control."

"I have made mistakes in the project because this project wasn't even for me in the first place. You don't have managing skills."

This blame game is very common in workplaces where unproductive people are trying to hide their worthlessness. The idea is to twist realities so that the manipulator shields his own faults by bringing the victim in the negative spotlight. All this time you try to figure out how it all became your fault, while the other person shifts the dirt from his shoulder to your shoulder.

3. Destroying your confidence

"You are doing great, but great isn't good enough."

A manipulator wants to keep hitting you and shaking your ground, but if you reach close to your expectations, it can make you confident so they also pull you down from time to time to destroy your confidence.

No matter how good you are, or how logical you sound, your thoughts and deeds will never get appreciated. Even if they do, the appreciation will come with a flaw.

You handle your home and work here as well. Wow, impressive!

But, isn't it easier for single people to manage work and home?

You live alone, right?

Oh! You have parents living with you.

Aren't you too old to live with your parents?

A married life builds character and teaches responsibility.

You shouldn't get married; otherwise, you will lose your professional focus.

These are the kind of conversations you can experience with a manipulator. They can define your whole personality by your marital status. Your hard work, qualifications, and success won't matter. This is the devilish power a manipulator can have over you.

4. Hurtful jokes and cruel sarcasm

"You took 5 hours to complete this evaluation. A blind child can do it better in half the time you spent."

Hurtful jokes and cruel sarcasm come your way when you are not suspecting them. In fact, you expect praise or at least someone to notice your effort; however, a manipulator uses such opportunities to look cleverer than you and make you look like a fool.

Generally, manipulators pass sarcastic comments when other people are present. Others laugh which validates the statement of the manipulator and ruins your moment of shining. Manipulators do it deliberately, while some people have a sarcastic nature, which they unconsciously use to destroy your ability to work in the office.

Have you prepared the presentation I asked this morning?

Oh! You have. Then, what are you waiting for, Christmas? Mail that presentation to my ID.

Have you ever sent an email to anyone? CC boss, boss' wife, Boss' servant, and Boss' dog. In fact, CC this whole office in the mail.

When such sarcastic comments are thrown your way, working gets difficult. You feel negative the moment you enter your office and that negative feeling doesn't allow you to stay productive or give your best while working.

5. Playing victim

"This whole office is against me. You are my only hope."

These are generally your team members and co-workers who play this card. You feel for these people because you actually see that they are being treated badly. Somehow, you are always around when these people are crying about their hard work not being paid. You know their problems and understand why they have not been able to complete the work. You pity them so much that you offer your service to help them out.

"My grandmother is in hospital. My parents are there, but my granny wants to see me only. Can you please finish this presentation for me, but don't send it to the boss, email it to me."

Guess what? You have fallen for this and now it is 7 in the evening and you are still in the office working. Plus, this hard work will not pay you anything. You would be lucky to get a thank you publicly. A *"thank you"* message will reach your mobile phone's inbox. That's it!

6. Covert threats

"You don't know what I am capable of in this office."

Covert threats start with small things, such as a harsh comment on your dressing sense, but, if you ignore it, these covert threats become more serious with time. You start hearing statements that start with "How dare you...," or, "Don't you listen..." and other cruel and threatening ways. Manipulators use their strong words and tone of voice to intimidate. Your boss and seniors can have this habit. They don't know how to respectfully treat juniors. Their behavior is polite when they are around their seniors but, with you, they behave like a dictator.

Threats begin in two major conditions. One is when you stay grounded and unaffected by all other methods of manipulation; then the manipulators decide to use language and other indirect ways to threaten you. They can threaten your job and even attack your whole career, but, generally, they attack your personal sensitivities.

Another condition is when you allow them to make threats. Not pointing out their harsh tone of voice is the biggest mistake an employee makes because, after a while, they use the same harsh voice tone every time you interact with them.

For instance, if you say, "Sir! Ms. Martha is calling you."

He might shout, "DON'T YOU HAVE ANY PATIENCE TO WAIT UNTIL I COMPLETE THIS WORK?"

And remember, no matter how hard you try to be perfect for them, these people will find something to shout about and threaten you with. In the process of trying to become better, you end up giving your emotional control over to these manipulating beasts.

7. Alternating your reality

"It is nothing but your imagination."

Making you question yourself is classic way manipulators try in an office. If you aren't confident about the things you see, feel or hear, you start depending on the manipulator to make decisions. A co-worker, a senior and even a junior can have this manipulative control over you. Anything that you say is turned into an imaginary reality of your own. This technique affects your personality, professional expertise and even your reputation in the office.

So what if I presented your project? I have done everything you asked. It is your own insecurity.

You might have already experienced many instances where people tried questioning your own realities. Make sure it doesn't happen anymore.

8. Irrelevant blaming

"If you do not give me this promotion, you're sexist."

For a manipulator, every office day is a mission in which he or she wants to conquer others and overpower them. Whether it is a simple conversation or a meeting, manipulators keep trying sabotaging your image, and irrelevant blaming is one of the many weapons they use. This technique is used to take an interaction to a whole new dimension.

For instance, if you are not ready to promote a female employee, you immediately become a feminist for this manipulator. The idea is to hit your sensitive side hard enough so you diverge from the actual motive of a conversation. The frustration hits and you start guarding yourself instead of presenting actual facts relevant to the conversation.

Stay in such an environment for long and you will lose your self-confidence. Your image will be twisted and your thoughts will become less important with time.

6 Different Kinds of Workplace Manipulators and How to Deal With Them

Manipulators make you doubt your senses and even ignore them. According to the manipulation technique used, there are 6 major types of workplace manipulators:

1. The drama creators

A drama creator has an over-the-top answer for everything you say. Such people in your office use exaggerations to manipulate your emotions. If you question such a manager about his bad performance in a project, the answer would be, "I have given my blood for this company all these years, and now you have the audacity to question my judgment." During all this, you think how to counter his "blood" argument. This leads to a retreat and you try to stay away from the person; hence, the manipulator gets away with anything he or she wants to do.

These drama creators are also there when you are not even trying to interrupt their way. If you ask such a manipulative boss, "I have a vacation plan with my family next week." The answer can be, "Yes! This company needs to work around your plans."

How to deal: To deal with such drama creators, you need factual intelligence. Always follow and present facts whenever talking to these people.

For example:

If your boss says, "This company doesn't work according to your personal plans."

You can say, "When joining, I was given the right to have vacations if I apply in advance."

Don't apologize if you are not on the wrong side of the conversation. This will allow the manipulator to cave you further. Any time a manipulator tries to exaggerate a situation, bring them back to the normal scenario with factual arguments.

For instance:

"You don't trust my 10 years of experience in this company."

You can reply:

"I do trust information that surrounds this project right now."

Do not engage by confirming the manipulator's hard work for the company. It might be true that the person has given many years to that company, but it is not relevant if he or she is not able to perform in a particular position.

Apart from this one scenario, you can get exposed to various drama creators in everyday work. Notice the signs and bring the dramatist to the factual level of conversation.

2. The distorter

These are probably the most common yet dangerous manipulators you might find in your workplace. They do not use emotions like drama creators. Distorted facts are their weapon of destruction. They gain information from all directions and become completely aware of everything going around. Then, they start leaking information and facts in a controlled manner to ensure you perceive what they want.

In a nutshell, the distorters are out there to mislead you by altering the reality you see. Mispresenting a scenario allows these manipulators to control your actions and decisions.

A colleague can tell you, *"I heard how our team leader was talking to the boss about you. I don't think he likes you."*

Or, a junior can tell you, *"Have you been going to a shrink? They don't say, but people are questioning your capabilities in this office. I think you should do something about it."*

Similarly, there are many situations when these manipulators merge their toxic thought with a fact, to destroy your ability to think correctly.

How many times have you delayed your business decisions because a subordinate promised you a big deal? A few distorted pieces of information felt as if the sales team is about to gain a big deal so you decided to wait for six months and allowed this time for the sales head. In the end, it was nothing but a tactic to overcome the shortfall in sales.

How to deal: A distorter gains comprehensive information and then distorts it so, to save yourself, you need to gain comprehensive information as well. Stop following what people say and conduct research on your own. Whether it is something work related or something related to your reputation in the office. Always be on top of everything. Verify facts before taking any action.

If a person gives you information even when you don't ask, find the real intentions. That person can be your well-wisher or a manipulator who just wants to persuade and use you. An intense inquiry is the only way to save yourself from such manipulators. Using multiple sources will help you find the loopholes in the manipulator's information, and then you can figure out who is the distorter in your workplace.

3. The attention diverter

This manipulator has the capability to shift an ongoing conversation according to his or her priorities. If a topic threatens to shine his or her faults, the manipulator smoothly changes the topic. These people are skilled in making irrelevant things seem relevant.

"I found some mistakes in the budget report you sent last week."

To this, a diverter can say, *"Man! The whole country is finding mistakes in the budget these days. Anyway, I'll get back to you."*

If you respond to their conversation diverting statements, these people can easily get out of any situation. As a result, you can face failure in your job and end up with bad consequences.

The attention diverter also knows about you. These people read your emotions and habits, so they learn how to divert your attention to other scenarios. They would know if you feel conscious about your reputation in the workplace or how seriously you handle your duties. They can use your personality traits or insecurities to their advantage.

How to deal: Your insecurities are your own and your emotions stay with you. However, it is up to you how much you allow other people to see those habits and emotions. Whenever you find someone trying to divert your attention, call out. Insist and force the conversation to stay relevant and talk about the real problems at hand.

You need to learn to concentrate whenever your mind feels insecure in a conversation. The diverter shouldn't get the chance to take your mind away from the actual topic.

For example, you can say:

"Don't change the topic. I want to finish this issue first."

You can use a mild tone or a harsh one when saying this, depending on the situation. Some manipulators require a minor sign to understand that you are not ready to be manipulated; however, others might require a strong repel from you in order back down.

4. The defamer

A person who is ready to put his or her faults on others comes under this category. A defamer merges the capability of diversion and distortion to manipulate the blame towards others. Such a manipulator can even try to not understand something or deliberately confuse two things as one. With that, they put the blame on others in a subtle way.

A defamer, when asked about the faulty strategy, can say, "I followed the format and guidelines given to me." They present such a vague argument that you can't comprehend the blame game. They use their acquisitions as general information so your focus shifts towards other people who come under a cycle of a decision.

Every office and every activity goes from one hand to the other so defamers don't need to put much effort in to defame others.

"All my customer service related decisions depend on the instructions he/she gives me."

"I send emails straight to her, so it is her responsibility to inform me about the required changes in the work patterns."

These statements are commonly used by defamers who either don't understand their job or don't want to do it properly.

How to deal: You need patience and problem-solving skills. You have to learn to analyze the chain of command and find the right culprit. Also, start noticing whether a person is genuinely not able to reason or is just pretending. You need to break from the deception and avoid the blame without getting affected by lies or wrong facts or hurting others.

You can say:

"If they are at fault, you are too."

Convey that the blame game won't work with you at all, and if someone tries to defame your work or reputation, call them out. Let them know that you have complete control over your work. Confidence and straight-forward conversations are the best techniques to stop such manipulators.

5. The bully

Such a manipulator has an aggressive response to any question you ask, especially if you question their work. When discussing work methods and strategies, you see such manipulators shouting the most. Ask them about their shortcomings and you see aggressive actions.

When asked about the negative sales, a bullying manager might stand up and shout, "Look at the numbers before saying anything." This is just one scenario, but you can see such behavior in many cases. Even if you are polite when asking the question, a bully always responds in a harsh manner. Their goal is to ensure that you leave them alone and don't ask the same thing again. They want to intimidate you and catch you by surprise.

How to deal: You should always stand firm in front of aggressive reactions. Don't let a bully bluff you with their harsh behavior. Keep yourself calm and present a non-nonsense argument to prove your point. The manipulator will keep giving aggressive reactions for a while, but you have to stay direct and don't allow them to affect you.

Aggression in a workplace is conquerable if you remind yourself about the sense of duty. A bully feels strongly about his or her reputation so, if you say, "This is not the way to behave in a professional environment," or, "You are acting completely opposite from our work culture," then these things would allow you to overpower the manipulator's manipulation.

Bullies usually attack their juniors in a workplace. If you come across a similar situation, say, "I will not respond until you talk to me with respect." Steal the option of being aggressive from a bully. This way, they won't get control over your sensitivities.

6. The criticizer

Criticism's impact on a person depends on the scenario. Sometimes, criticism can induce growth and allow a professional to grow, but those criticisms aren't too direct. On the other hand, there are manipulators who use criticism to control your actions and behavior. The goal of a criticizer is not to improve your skills. In fact, he or she wants you to stay bad at your job so that they can keep criticizing you. These criticizers can attack you, even if you are good at your job. These people find something to make you feel inferior and reduce your self-esteem.

Using contempt, labels, and judgments, a criticizer questions your character and personality. They are usually very direct. "Criticism improves your performance." The manipulator hides behind this perception and says anything he or she wants to say.

As a result, such a manipulator makes you feel under-confident and ashamed.

How to deal: A manipulator will always have something to criticize you. It is your job to understand people in your office who are always ready to criticize you one way or the other. These people will come around you to criticize you. If you finish your report on time, they criticize you for the quality of work and say that you are too hasty and unfocused. It is always something or the other for them.

So, you need to stop taking them seriously, and then tell them, "I will accept this same criticism if you say it politely." Don't let them disrespect you. Also, allow relevant criticism only. Don't let manipulators talk about your personal habits or personal life in a criticizing manner. Remind them that they don't have any authority over your life.

All types of manipulators share one thing. They all stand in front of your inner-self and the outer world. They create false realities and play with your perceptions. You get fooled only if your inner-self is not in sync with you. Understand your emotional strengths and weaknesses. You need to train your mind and learn to own your emotions. With that, you can avoid getting manipulated by such manipulators.

Leaving your job is not a solution. All the above-mentioned manipulators are out there in every work environment. You will have to face them everywhere. In fact, it becomes difficult to understand manipulators in a new environment; hence, you should trust yourself and focus on getting stronger in terms of emotions and perceptions. Know how your inner-self works and hold the steering wheel in your hands. Don't allow another person to drive you crazy and let you act according to his or her ideas.

CHAPTER 5 - Manipulation In Relationships And How To Avoid It

The first year of the relationship was like a dream come true for Teresa. Matt was everything she had ever dreamed of. They went for holidays together, and Matt even attended thanksgiving with Teresa's parents but, after that one year of a perfect relationship, things started to get a little difficult. Matt began to literally command Teresa for things. He asked for money, used her place for parties and stopped giving her attention. Every time Teresa refused for something, Matt fought and gave her the silent treatment for days. As Teresa wanted those old lovely days back, she tried everything possible to keep Matt happy.

It took another 2 years of a messy relationship for Teresa to realize one morning that she was under the control of Matt.

Manipulation in a relationship is a great issue for people, and it doesn't only happen in a partner relationship. A family member or a friend can also twist and control your emotions. These masters of manipulation ruin your ability to think, act and feel at your own will. You experience what they want you to experience and you act under their influence. You live in a false hope of achieving a perfect relationship with that person; hence, it takes a long time to realize that you are being manipulated.

To save you from such manipulations, you will find three separate evaluations of relationships here:

·   Partner or love relationship
·   Family relationship
·   Friend's relationship

Let's begin with the first one!

Partner or Love Relationship Manipulation – How It Works And Things You Can Do

Manipulation is defined mostly as a deliberate action taken by people; however, in love relationships, people tend to manipulate each other unintentionally and intentionally as well. No matter what, manipulation in a partner relationship is always toxic for your mind and life.

Here are all the signs of a manipulative partner:

1. The territory advantage

Are you living your life or your partner's? A love relationship is about sharing your life, but manipulative partners tend to bring you into their life and disconnect you with your own life before the relationship.

Think about:

Do you live in your partner's apartment?

How many times do you go out to your favorite spots?

If your partner's friends are yours, then does your partner meet your friends too?

Taking you in their own surroundings allows manipulators to control you. As you don't understand that surrounding, you decide according to your partner's will.

For example, if you go to your partner's favorite restaurant, you would say, "You come here often, so pick what we should order." Such simple things slowly condition you to hand over your emotional and personality buttons to your partner.

How to save yourself: In the beginning, you don't know whether your partner is a manipulator or just shy to share your life, but you need to test him/her. Make your relationship a 50-50 exchange. Share elements of your partner's life, but also encourage him or her to do things which you like. Clarify that you are committed only if the relationship is equal and healthy.

For instance, if your partner asks to go to a restaurant, say, "Ok, we can go, but next week I will pick the restaurant and you can't say no or cancel the night." Follow a similar attitude of equality in all parts of your relationship.

2. Playing your sensitivities

How many times have you done something because your partner said, "I know you're kind enough to understand?"

Let's consider a scenario:

Suppose your partner wants to shop for a new designer dress or a bike, but he or she is short on money. The right way of asking for money would be requesting you and assuring that you will get the money back. If you explain the financial problems, a genuine partner would understand, but a manipulator won't care about your problems. They would try to twist your affection with something like, "Don't you love me enough to give me some money?" or, "What is more important, money or me? Let's clear this out today." This is a combination of love and force, to play your sensitivity and affection.

How to save yourself: First of all, allow your mind to feel that not following your partner's desires doesn't make you a bad or insensitive person.

Then, you should think of a balanced decision and come up with a reasonable alternative. For the given situation above, you can say, *"My love for you and my money are two different things. You know I would help you if it was possible right now."*

Replying this way, you would ensure that your sensitivities aren't clouding your decisions in a relationship.

3. Dramatic blackmailing

Blackmailing is the most common reason why a relationship turns unhealthy. You start hearing things like, "I will do something to myself if you don't come right now," or, you can hear, "I can't live a single day without you."

Blackmailing comprises a variety of manipulative tactics such as shame, guilt, and fear as well. A manipulative partner can deliberately get hurt and say, "Why weren't you there to save me?" You feel guilty and ashamed of your ignorance. All your attention goes to your partner and the relationship becomes your whole life.

Such a relationship does nothing but ruin your life. You become responsible towards your partner too much, which doesn't allow you to follow your own dreams or lifestyle.

How to save yourself: Such manipulators begin with simple blackmailing to condition your mind. If you promote the initial behavior, it can lead to extreme levels of blackmailing.

If you are already facing dramatic blackmailing, don't get scared. Instead, counter the person with a logical reply like, "If you try anything to harm yourself, I will call the police. We can go to a psychiatrist, but don't expect me to deal with this behavior." It might seem a cruel thing to say, but that's the only way to handle a dramatic manipulator.

4. Self-victimization

No matter how wrong your partner is, you are the one apologizing every single time. Does this happen to you whenever you fight with your partner?

If your partner doesn't apologize ever for anything, it's a sign. Such people always make you the culprit and become a victim on their own.

You are arguing, "How could you take my money without asking me?" But the answer will be, "You are shouting just for a few bucks. Why do you always find a way to hurt my feelings and ruin my day?"

So, the mistake of your partner vanishes and the topic moves to your reaction. You are the one who hurt and broke your partner's heart so it is your responsibility to apologize and you end up saying, "I am so sorry baby, I didn't mean to hurt you like that."

How to save yourself: Remember one thing! Apologize only after self-evaluating your mistake. Your partner can make you feel ashamed with self-victimization. You need to carefully assess those situations and don't let the bluff work on you.

If your partner complains about your raised voice or hurtful blames, politely reply, "I apologize for the way I reacted, but you should apologize too. What you have done is wrong on so many levels."

Your partner might try to melt you with tears. Stay there to show your compassion without diverting from your point.

5. Toxic jokes

Manipulative partners criticize, hurt and then say, "I am just kidding. Stop making such a big scene." You feel like you are overreacting to something that means nothing, but that "fun" loving nature of your partner can be a manipulation. Public criticism is usually a way to get control over your behavior. Your partner can say, "Look how she dances," so you don't dance with anyone at that party. You can't react; otherwise, you will be ruining the party for everyone. Such manipulators don't stop from raising their voice if you reply anything.

The same manipulation technique is used privately as well. A manipulative partner learns your insecurities and then attacks them in private to win an argument or control your actions.

"Hello? Is it you or your mom talking? I have read those childhood things you have written in your diary."

How to save yourself: Taking a stand for yourself is a necessity. No matter how funny a comment is and who is making that comment, you should call it out. Stay humble, but make sure that the partner knows you don't appreciate such jokes.

You can say, *"Please don't make a comment like this ever. I don't find it funny at all."*

Call your partner out, *"Are you trying to make me feel bad?"*

"Then, stop saying such hurtful things."

If you shut the person immediately, they won't crack such toxic jokes in future. Or even if they still do, then you know where you stand with them and that makes it clearer on how to handle them.

6. Using society to sell you an idea

We all try to feel a part of a society. The society includes everyone you know outside your blood relations. Your partner can use society as a reference to convince you for something. Social obligations are one of the biggest responsibilities that people feel in their life. So, when your partner says, "Our friends go out for vacation at least twice every year," you think and feel obligated to do the same.

Similarly, your partner can say, "Every wife in our neighborhood has more than 10 designer dresses. You can give me at least 2." Such an argument makes two designer dresses seem logical. After all, others have more than 10 you know! Such manipulation is not always deliberate, but you should have the knowledge to notice it.

How to save yourself: Your partner is using references of others to convince you for things you won't allow otherwise. First of all, evaluate how many times you let such manipulation happen in your daily life. If it is once or twice in a long time, then there is no need to worry about it, but, if it happens very often, then it highlights two things: One is that your partner is trying to manipulate you in order to get things done, and the second is that you are vulnerable towards social obligations.

In order to save yourself, you need to modify how you see society. Control your inner-self and don't allow society to become a huge part of your decision-making process. With that, you will become capable of saying "no" to your partner on such obligations.

7. *Neutralizing wrong behavior by giving untrue reasons*

Alternative story creation is what this manipulation is all about. Your partner gets caught for doing something wrong, but, instead of apologizing, he or she might create a new story of lies in which those actions are justified. The story would be so believable that you would end up praising your partner for an intelligent action.

For instance, if your partner is caught cheating, he or she might say:

"You are not there anymore! Your work has become everything for you. I know you do it for us, but I am a human, and I desire attention."

"I hope you understand...."

"That was the only way possible..."

"Circumstances made me do it...."

That is how a partner tries to justify his or her behavior.

Even if you don't praise them, they try at least neutralizing their wrong behavior with distorted reasons. They create a reality in which circumstances made him or her do those wrong things.

How to save yourself: Your partner is either using lies or distorting the scenarios so you need to break the barrier of lies first. For that, you need to ask questions. Don't let one action justify another. You can say:

"If I was doing something wrong, you could have talked to me. Why didn't you?"

"Why didn't you explain things to me?"

"This, right here, is your entire fault. Don't try to put the blame on me."

"Why didn't you ask for my opinion on this? How am I supposed to understand this wrong behavior now?"

It is like a light interrogation, which cops do on culprits. If you question long enough, liars start spitting the truth because they can't keep up the same story format.

8. Passive aggression

Your partner agrees to something first but then the silence begins. An upset facial expression stays on all the time until you do as your partner desires. This is how passive aggression feels like.

Such manipulators stop talking or talk only a little to convey that they are upset. To avoid this, you end up agreeing with your partner. However, your partner would say, "You are doing this on your own. I have given my permission to you." The idea is to convince you without asking for it. A manipulative partner knows how much you love him/her but still, they don't want to seem demanding. Their passive aggression allows them to fight the fight.

Suppose your partner asked you to move in to live together. You discussed it and explained that you don't feel ready to move in at that stage. Your partner says, "It's completely fine," and things move on. However, suddenly, your calls are being ignored, and your partner is not available to meet. Even when you are together, your partner doesn't seem interested in being with you. It goes on until you propose the idea of moving in together on your own.

Just imagine, your partner didn't say a word directly, but convinced you to do what he/she wanted. That is how this manipulation tactic works.

How to save yourself: A partner, who constantly does this to you, doesn't deserve your love so control your heart first. Then, you can counter with something like, *"I am disappointed with your childish behavior. I know what you are trying to do and it won't work at all."*

Make your partner realize that your love doesn't make you a weak person. Stand up with compassion and confidence.

"I will be there for you always, but you have to respect my decisions if you really love me."

9. Active aggression

This manipulation is easily visible if it happens. You can see the aggression in their actions, voice, and expressions.

For instance, your partner asks you to make breakfast, but you say, "I don't feel like it." In return, you face an aggressive voice saying, "Don't ruin my day or I don't know what I'll do with you." So, you go and prepare the breakfast in order to avoid any fight. This motivates the manipulator to attack you with aggressive behavior more often. Whenever you aren't ready to do something or agree, your partner uses aggression to force those things on you.

This mean behavior can even lead to something dangerous. Manipulators with narcissistic tendencies start hurting their partners physically if not stopped. Eventually, these things happen for no reason at all, just to showcase power and keep you under control.

How to save yourself: This part is a little tricky. If the manipulator is really aggressive, it would be wise to do as he or she says in the present, but you should find an escape eventually. If your partner hasn't reached the physical level of abuse, you can say "no" and show that you are not afraid of him/her.

The ultimate solution is to get out of such a relationship as quickly as possible. Find an escape and file complaints against physical abuse of any such kind.

Family relationship manipulation - how it works and things you can do

Wouldn't you feel surprised to find out that your loved ones are manipulating you? Manipulation in a partner relationship is common; however, people usually skip the sight of a manipulative father, mother, brother or a sister as well.

The desire to control one another drives family members to manipulate each other with physical, mental, emotional and even sexual abuse. A family member with a manipulative nature and a false sense of pride tries to rule the home like his or her own kingdom. In such a situation, other family members become small instruments for the manipulator, which he or she controls as pleased.

Why is it Hard to Understand Mental Manipulation in the Family?

You grow up in your family surrounded by the thoughts, actions, and behaviors of other members. Staying with them conditions your mind towards their abusive behavior; hence, your mind doesn't even realize that you are being manipulated. For you, it is a normal household scenario that happens every weekend.

This is what doesn't allow people to decipher mental manipulation. Such people realize the mental manipulation after getting out, and stay away from the family for a while.

You don't have to feel threatened. Here are a few signs to help you understand all kinds of family relationship manipulation and things you can do to save yourself:

1. Lying, even if it is not required

To protect ourselves from shame and embarrassment, we tend to lie in many situations to our own family members. Sometimes, you lie just to keep your loved ones away from concerns. All these scenarios are justifiable because they happen once in a long time.

However, a manipulative family member can lie on a daily basis for no reason at all, but they will give you a legitimate reality where they are right to lie. This will happen regularly for small things.

Let's go through a scenario:

When Kate gave money to her younger brother for the electricity bill, she informed him about the last date for paying the bill.

The next day, Kate asked her brother, "Have you paid the bill, Sam?"

To that, he said, "Yes, I have."

But on the last day of paying the bill, all the lights went off.

When Kate inquired again, her brother vaguely replied, "I had something urgent to do, so I used that money. You give me money now and I will get that money back soon."

The problem was that Kate has been dealing with this behavior of her brother for a very long time. He does it again and again. If he wants something from Kate's room, he takes it without asking. In fact, he denies if Kate asks for that thing. Most of the time, Kate finds her lost things in her brother's room only. Now, she usually starts with his room whenever she loses her stuff.

A manipulator lies and then replies vaguely if you question them. They are ready to tell multiple lies over and over again.

How to save yourself: If you are dealing with such a family member, it will require patience. You know the behavior, so stop offering important responsibilities to them. Also, tell them, "I am here to help you no matter what, but that won't happen if you lie to me." Point out their lies in front of other family members and slowly motivate them to lose this habit.

2. The disguised selflessness

Some family members are honorable, while some just imitate as caring individuals. Selflessness can be an act of a manipulator in your family. Statements like, "Have I done anything for myself in this family?" are heard from such manipulators. The difference between real selfless people and disguising manipulators is that the latter one reminds you about his or her selflessness very often. The moment they see you getting free from their clutches, they say, "All I did was for you, and this is how you pay me!" Comments like this attack your guilt and sensitivities and you end up giving your control to that person.

How to save yourself: First of all, you need to realize that people who praise their selflessness are not selfless at all, and such a manipulator can be very close to you, which is why protection becomes difficult. But you can say, "I admire everything that you have done for me and this family, but I am old enough to make my own decisions now."

3. Intimidation and physical abuse

Sometimes, family relationships get ugly with straightforward threats and physical abuse. An intimating father, mother or a sibling can turn your life into hell. These manipulators don't believe in indirect methods of manipulation. They create fear with actual physical abuse, threats and intimidating actions.

How to save yourself: Just like an abusive partner, you need to find a way out from the life of an abusive family member. Find any way to escape without making them realize that you are trying to leave them. After getting a safe environment, you should file a complaint against such a family member.

4. Shaming

Family members know about our weaknesses and protect them, but a manipulative family member would use those weaknesses of yours to bully and make you feel ashamed. Shaming to blackmail or just to get control over you is common. The manipulator wants you to act according to his or her instructions.

How to save yourself: It is all about building your own self-esteem. These manipulators work your insecurities so, if you conquer them, the manipulator will have nothing to play with. Remind yourself that everyone has one of the other weaknesses. In fact, learn to flaunt your weaknesses on your own. This way, you will own your personality truly. That's what real confidence is.

Friendship Manipulation - How It Works And Things You Can Do?

Do you feel as if you are the one always giving something to a friend? You agree whenever that friend asks you to go out, but that person is always busy when you need him/her. If so, then there is a chance you are dealing with a manipulative friend.

A one-sided friendship is another form of manipulation you can come across. Some friends find it amusing to control people and use them as their puppets. Such manipulations can begin at the school level and go on for life.

If you make a narcissistic person your best friend, things are bound to go south for you.

Here is how manipulative friends work:

1. They constantly try to control you

A manipulative friend wants you to follow his or her ideas. Whenever you are around that person, you feel like you are being controlled. Such a friend chooses places to hang out alone and you are supposed to follow them. They can even try to control your dressing style, your personal decisions, and other relationships as well. Such a manipulative friend acts like a guide in your life, but, actually, they are just enjoying your vulnerability.

How to save yourself: Find a pattern of a manipulative friend. Look how many times your friend questions your judgment and tries to force his or her point of view. If you see clear signs of being controlled, stand up for yourself. You should say, "I am capable of making my own decisions."

2. They ignore you

Having a conversation with a manipulative friend has no meaning. A manipulative friend doesn't really care about you so, if the conversation is not interesting to them, they won't listen. For instance, you had a bad day at work and you are now sharing that experience with your friend. A manipulative friend would look away, keep using his or her phone, or interrupt you in the middle of the conversation and change the topic.

How to save yourself: Realize that your friend has no concern for what happens in your life. Evaluate this behavior and call them out, "I am talking to you. Please focus or let me know if you are not interested." This will not allow them to take you for granted.

3. They always need a favor

You help your friend once because of the relationship but then, the behavior gets repeated again and again. The manipulative friend tests your extent of kindness by asking for little favors at first. They can ask, "Can you give me your car for 30 minutes?" or, "Do you have an extra dress for me? I have nothing good to wear." Eventually, these little favors increase to larger scales, for example, "Please lend me 10,000 bucks, and I will pay you next month." If you motivate such behavior, such a manipulative friend will keep using you.

How to save yourself: Learn to say "No." Whenever you are asked for a favor, you should think, "What was the last time I helped this person?" and, "How much this favor is going to cost me?" If you find the situation not comfortable for you, politely refuse to help with a legitimate reason, such as, "This is not the right time for me to help you."

4. They use emotional defense

Just like a partner, a manipulative friend can also use emotions to play you for a fool. If you confront, they tend to act in a defensive way, and their defense involves an emotional attack. They can blame you for hurting them emotionally.

How to save yourself: Whenever you find yourself in an emotional attack, stay calm. The manipulator would try to resist the conversation, so, you should say, "We need to talk about this whether you like it or not." They can try to make you feel guilty, so you should read such signs too. Don't feel sorry for the person just because he or she wants you to. Make sure the conversation stays on topic.

5. They tend to bully a lot

Best friends make fun of each other, but a manipulator doesn't take jokes, as he/she just wants to make fun of you. A manipulator would bully you more in front of others. They have a need to present themselves superior to you in every scenario. This is their inner-complexities and insecurities that motivate them to behave this way.

How to save yourself: Sit your friend down and explain things clearly, "I don't know whether you do it deliberately, or without knowing, but I am not going to take your jokes anymore." Become firm and take a stand for yourself. If your friend still doesn't back down, it is time to put an end to that friendship.

6. They are nowhere to be found when you need them

These friends appear in your life once in a while only. Whenever they do, they desire something from you. After you fulfill their desire, they vanish without giving you any clue. You try to call and get in touch, but they are always busy, and their social media profiles are always filled with pictures of places where he/she goes to hang out with other friends.

How to save yourself: These people are not your friend at all. You just need to stop giving them any attention immediately.

A manipulative friend attacks the same emotional vulnerabilities as your partner and family members so it all comes down to taking care of yourself. You should learn self-love and give priority to yourself. Make every relationship a 50-50 give and take exchange. This way, you will earn the respect you deserve and the satisfaction of being in a healthy relationship.

Don't ignore the signs. Your intuitions tell you everything about a bad relationship. Act on those signs and find true people to have relationships with.

CHAPTER 6 – Get Into Their Heads. Know Thyself And Also Know These Manipulators

Don't you think how a person could deliberately try to control other people? We all are taught to believe in the goodness of people, but then the reality brings us to the ground with manipulators who can easily become the master of our inner-self with their deceptions.

A manipulator sees the world in a different way. In fact, it would not be wrong to say that manipulators understand life and people better than an ordinary person does. However, they use this ability to con and deceive people to get what they want.

In the mind of a manipulator, the whole world is a big board game of chess. They see you as an expendable tool. On the outside, they will give you care, love and protection, but this protection and affection are only there because you are useful to them.

Believe or not, a manipulator begins his or her observations by learning their own insecurities. They decipher their own emotional problems and evaluate the reasons behind it. This gives them the insight over how emotions affect our actions. With that insight, they observe other people on a daily basis. Your facial expressions, your reactions towards things, and your words help them learn about you. Things that you say and things that you don't, it all gives some insight to a skilled manipulator.

Using your emotional state and personality characteristics, a manipulator molds his or her personality accordingly. They can act like a very different person in front of two different people. For you, they are fun loving and outgoing, but, for some other person, they can be a victim of unfortunate incidents. They love creating stories and building a character that aligns with their victims so, if they feel something, you feel that same emotion too. It happens due to the strong bond a manipulator forms with the victim. This bond can include intimidation, love, authority, victimization, guilt, friendship, kindness and other emotions. This way, manipulators control your thoughts and make you see reality as they desire.

They Enjoy Tricking People

A con artist likes fooling people into giving him/her money or other things. For manipulators, manipulation is an art which they enjoy. They feel rewarded when you do as they say, or think exactly how they want you to. If a manipulator wants you to feel scared, he or she will use shame, bullying, lying and other tricks to make you feel that way. When you do, it would give the manipulator a rush they crave.

Manipulators score themselves whenever they win or lose. They have their own justifications for their actions.

"If you are so open, the world will use you at every step. Why not me?"

"I am using my talents to win what I want, and having some fun in the way as well! Everyone does that."

"Everyone is trying to manipulate each other. I am just good at it."

Their justifications are good enough reasons for them to manipulate people and don't care about them. These justifications further enhance the pleasure of control and tricking people. Manipulators define their lives around their ability to make others do things for them.

They Do Everything to Win

Every move, every word and every action of a manipulator is well-calculated. They might not always win, but their intentions are towards the victory every single time. Manipulators want every single person around them to submit control. Whether it is a love relationship or a corporate colleague, the goal is to find vulnerabilities in people and use them to manipulate. In fact, they can even use your personality strengths against you. For instance, if a person tries to be happy instead of all the bad things happening around, a manipulator can paint an altered happy picture of life to get the submission.

The techniques depend on the purpose of manipulating the victims. A manipulator can be charming or a big bully, depending on what he or she wants from you. That's the reason how some partners become a completely different person at different phases of a relationship. They seem charming at first because they want the other person to fall in love. As the relationship goes on, they desire control over the actions of their partner; hence, the blackmailing, silent treatments and intimidation begin.

A manipulator has more than one mask and he/she will try each one of them to win.

They Have Sharp Communication Skills

Communication skill is the biggest weapon used by a manipulator. Victims don't even realize when words impact their subconscious and conscious mind.

A good communicator is not always a manipulator, but a manipulator is always a good communicator. Their communication skills include:

- Their command over words.
- Their ability to say vague statements as facts.
- Their confidence when arguing or lying.
- Their ability to use sarcasm and irony.

If you come to confront a manipulator about a disrespectful statement, the manipulator can make that statement feel like a compliment to you. Similarly, they can wrap their hurtful statements in a compliment.

"Wow! You have read Gautama Buddha. I thought you were a dumb girl, but you're not!"

They use language to shake the ground of their victims and comfort them whenever required. They can say the best things about you in one second, and turn them into insults in another. It is all to grab your reactions on different scenarios, which allows them to read you better.

All in all, their insults hurt and their compliments melt your heart. That's how communication allows a manipulator to get out of any situation and create different scenarios.

They Look for the Scope of Vulnerability

In the mind of a manipulator, every person is vulnerable. Just the extent of vulnerability differs from person to person. Less vulnerable people are difficult to manipulate, while high vulnerability makes a person an easy target. Many manipulators like to assess and attack less vulnerable people just to enjoy the game; however, they do it in only safe scenarios. Otherwise, their goal is to pick the most vulnerable and twist their emotions to get what they wish for.

So, for example, a person with a few friends would be a better target than a person with many friends. Similarly, manipulators judge the scope of vulnerability in terms of self-esteem, confidence level, career, happiness, desires, and hopes. If they get to choose, the most vulnerable personality will get attacked in a group of options.

They don't stop if they come across a firm-minded person. Their idea is that every person has hopes, no matter how happy or confident he or she is so they attack those hopes as vulnerabilities. The manipulator can lose as well, but a loss is a big pain and the manipulator tries again and again to ensure his/her victory.

They Fool Their Own Mind As Well

In order to lie with confidence and keep up their character, manipulators create stories. They work on those stories in detail and make them believable in their own mind as well. Even when they are lying, one part of their brain treats those lies as truths. That's how they flawlessly remember their stories and tell the same lie for years and years without changing a single detail. They think about every potential question against their story and prepare an answer for that. If someone tries to question them, they immediately present an answer. Eventually, those lies become a truth for the manipulator as well.

"Where did you spend your weekend?"

"Ah! In a great beachside resort with my girlfriend. It was magical."

"But you said you had some personal thing to take care of?"

"Yeah man! That personal thing was my lovely girlfriend's birthday. She has recently lost her father, so I wanted to give her a much-needed vacation."

After such a conversation, don't be surprised to find out that the guy doesn't even have a girlfriend. He wanted a vacation, so he took it, and then he wanted his colleagues to think of him as a caring family man, so he created the girlfriend and a whole story around that. Now, this girlfriend would get gifts and restaurant dates whenever this manipulator wants to ditch the office and go out.

10 Common Characteristics All Manipulators Possess

Every manipulator holds some personality traits he or she uses to control people, situations, and actions.

1. Self-protection

Manipulative people are driven by the idea of self-protection. To protect themselves, they can engage others because they can. Some manipulators don't know they have skills. It is only the sense of self-protection that drives them to manipulate people without knowing.

You can consider self-protection as a motive and manipulation as a technique. For every bad thing a manipulator does, self-protection becomes the legitimate reason, "I did it to protect myself from the world." As a result, abusers, controllers, and other manipulators don't question their actions ever. It is ultimately about their feelings, their motives, and their desires. Other people's emotions are just a way to get what a manipulator wants.

The instinct of self-protection is in every human being, but not every one of us possesses the skills of manipulation. The strong desire of protecting self-motives meets a manipulative mind to create a dangerous, manipulative personality. Such people truly believe in their actions, which is why manipulators are so fluent in rationalizing their bad actions. They can present an amazing reason for something that is completely out of line.

For a girl who manipulates her partner to gain power over his life, it is just self-protection. She would say something like this, "You don't know how difficult it is for a woman to live in this world. I did what I had to for survival." She will explain her life in a story where she has been a victim of this cruel world, and that the cruelty of the world makes her actions completely legitimate and right.

Similarly, manipulators use the weaknesses of society and people to play them. The characteristic of self-protection gives manipulators the confidence over their choices.

2. No regards for personal space

Manipulators, who don't know they are manipulators, lack the understanding of personal identity. On the other hand, manipulators who deliberately manipulate don't care about people's personal space. A manipulator attacks emotionally, physically, spiritually and psychologically as well. Sometimes they attack just one aspect of personal identity or, sometimes, they can also attack all aspects.

If the manipulation is forceful, the victim feels different stages of exhaustion. Abusers, intimidators and other direct manipulators demean the personal space and weaken their victims.

On the other hand, a subtle manipulation hurts at the end. The manipulator attacks the victim like a silent parasite and starts corrupting his or her psychology; however, the person doesn't realize that he/she is being manipulated. The realization period occurs after the manipulator leaves the personal space, which leaves people in a rage, feel regret, and other hurtful feelings.

Personal space of people is the working ground for manipulators. They can only hurt their victims by learning personal space and its elements. That is why every manipulator holds the ability to read people's personal identity. They observe the physical, mental, and emotional capabilities of people before manipulating them.

If you ask a manipulator about the personal space of people, they would say, "It is personal only if you live in isolation. People showcase their identities with their words and actions. So, how is that a personal identity?" A manipulator believes in accessing every door possible to learn about their victims because, if the door is accessible, one has the right to open it and go inside. That's how they feel entering into a victim's psychology to observe.

3. Self-confidence

A manipulative person is always confident about his or her actions and thoughts; however, they tend to show or hide their confidence as they please. It allows them to avoid taking responsibilities. They like other people to take responsibilities. This way, a manipulator can easily turn the blame to another person for his/her own actions. They work behind the scenes, but come out as a confident person if it benefits them. If taking responsibility suits their purpose, manipulators come forward to satisfy their own needs.

Whether they show their confidence or not, manipulators leave no room for their victim's survival. When playing a victim, a manipulator hides his or her confidence to make the character believable. On the other hand, a manipulator shows maximum levels of confidence when using intimidation, sarcasm or other methods of manipulation.

You can hear the same person say two different things on different days:

"I have no clue how to handle my money. Can we open a joint account?"

"I decide how I spend my money, what to shop for, where to go and what to wear. Don't try to control me."

The confidence level changes according to the scenario and motives of a manipulator, but that only happens on the outside. On the inside, that person has always been confident about his or her abilities so, in a way, self-confidence is not a trait. Instead, the ability to show or hide confidence is the true trait a manipulator holds.

4. Motivator

Manipulators have the ability to motivate people towards something. Their power over communication skills allows them to convey what a victim wants to hear. Manipulators understand a person's sensibilities and sensitivities. This way, they learn about how caring, kind, practical, or emotional a person is. Using this observation, manipulators start motivating the side they want to attack. For instance, if a person is insecure about his or her looks, a manipulator would praise their facial features.

"You have a desirable smile and your caring nature makes that smile more beautiful for me."

If they know the insecurities of a person, they praise in a subtle way with specific compliments so, instead of saying, "You are beautiful," they say, "Your eyes talk your beauty," plus they would combine this compliment with the person's kindness or caring nature. This way, the victim tends to buy those lies.

Similarly, a manipulator can motivate bad feelings in a person if he or she wants to. If a victim is feeling sad, a manipulator can motivate that sadness to fulfill a purpose. The same goes for fear, hope, anger, jealousy and other feelings that a person can struggle with.

The ability to motivate feelings is common in all types of manipulators. They use this characteristic to create a relationship and strengthen the bond with their victims.

5. Practical empathy

Empathy is the ability to understand other people's feelings and share those feelings, but a manipulator doesn't feel general empathy. Manipulators have a practical sense of empathy, which means they understand people's feelings without sharing them. A manipulator is like a robot looking at a happy or sad person. The feelings are visible to them, but they practically observe those feelings to fulfill their purpose.

If you talk to a manipulator about relationships in general, they usually tend to divide relationships into needs, wants and other practical aspects. They will tell you logical reasons why two people are in love with each other. If two celebrities marry each other, a manipulator would say how one celebrity is trying to climb up the ladder and the other is just trying to get over an old relationship.

Manipulative people see the dynamics in relationships such as intrigue, jealousy, rivalry, affection, attraction, hope, and need. They use these dynamics to play multiple people together and ruin the harmony between these people. They can encourage or discourage you to love someone or hate someone. It all depends on what means you fulfill, in their big plan.

6. Hidden insecurities

Behind all that confidence and charm hides an insecure person in a manipulator. Their ability to observe feelings allows them to understand their own insecurities as well; however, just like their self-confidence, they can hide their insecurities as well. Every time you see a manipulator victimizing himself, there is a certain level of truth in that.

They use their insecurities as well to mold into a character and fool people.

Sometimes, the insecurity drives manipulators towards vulnerable people. They want to gain attention and feel superior but, that would be possible only if they can find a person more vulnerable than them, so the search for vulnerable victims begins and people end up getting hurt in the process.

The insecure personality traits of a manipulator give him or her the obsessiveness towards their goals. In a relationship, an insecure, manipulative person tends to find reasons to blame the partner to hear apologies. Manipulators want their victims to follow their lead. Some manipulators desire praise, and some desire control over the victim. Also, the motives can change from victim to victim as well.

7. Multiple personalities

Manipulators are like chameleons. They have a tendency to change themselves depending on the situation they are in, or the person they want to persuade. Multiple personality traits live inside every person; however, not everyone deliberately hides or showcases those personalities to gain something but manipulators do that. They mold themselves to create a disguised persona in front of a victim so, if a manipulator wants you to feel scared, you will never see him or her laughing or talking to you in a light manner. It is a constant character play they perform. You think your boss or partner is very serious and scary, but the same person behaves completely different in other situations.

The ability to change personalities make manipulators extremely dangerous. In relationships, we tend to create a picture of our partners or friends, but what if that picture is all wrong? You see a perfect partner in front of you, while he or she is cheating on you and getting away with it.

When changing personalities, manipulators work on three aspects - behavior, opinions and feelings. They choose to behave in a certain way in front of certain people. They blend righteousness in their behavior to build trust in people. Manipulators can shake their victims with multiple behaviors on random days. A manipulative wife can choose to switch her mood often to keep her husband under control.

Manipulators can debate for or against at the same time. They present opinions in a vague manner so that no-one can hold them accountable for anything. Switching sides and opinions allows them to say exactly what a victim desires. If two different victims are talking to the manipulator at the same time, he or she can easily get out of the situation with a vague opinion, such as, "You both are saying some logical and intelligent things. We should keep an open mind to gain the best of both worlds."

In terms of feelings, manipulators can be ruthless. They have the ability to observe how a person is feeling. They use this skill to change their persona and convey their feelings accordingly. This means that if the victim has done something bad today and feeling remorse, a manipulator will use that remorse by acting like a victim. In remorse, a person desires to do something good, so manipulators use that to make victims do what they want.

8. Indirect communication

Although manipulators are great communicators, they like to use other people to convey what they desire. They will present themselves as if they are a straightforward person who talks what he thinks; however, they like to plant seeds in the mind of people. You won't even realize when a manipulator is making you his or her messenger. They fool you into thinking that their ideas are your ideas so, when you do it, the blame is on you, "Nobody put a gun to your head buddy! You came on your own."

They design their conversations in terms of questions and constantly ask whether you agree or don't. This way, they can always stay out of sight and get you to do exactly the way they want.

"Dude! Someone needs to do something about Damon. He is talking bad things about us everywhere in this office."

"What, really? I can't take it anymore. He will face me directly this time."

That's how a conversation happens with a manipulator. He or she plants a seed conveying the hidden message. The manipulator wants you to do his or her dirty work without even taking any part in it. After you act for them, they simply say you did it on your own; 'I just shared my feelings because I was concerned.'

Using other people as a messenger allows manipulators to hide themselves and get out of every situation. They create a scenario and look at everything from the outside. Nobody even suspects that it was them triggering each one of them and, even if people find out, manipulators hold other people accountable for their actions. In any scenario, they ensure their victory.

9. Jealousy

A manipulator won't admit it, but jealousy is a big part of their mindset. For many manipulators, it is the driving force that motivates them to play people's vulnerabilities. The feeling of jealousy comes from almost everything because manipulators desire to feel superior to everyone so a manipulator can feel jealous of his or her own parents, siblings, spouses and friends. The jealousy stays on until, and unless, they get control over that person. Holding a person's emotions and actions in hand, manipulators feel more powerful and better than the other person.

A manipulator can feel jealous of someone's money, so he or she can target the loneliness of that person. Similarly, a manipulator can feel jealous of someone's look, so he or she tries to sabotage that person's relationship. Anything good in your life, whether it is physical or emotional, can make a manipulator jealous and they can choose to destroy that good feeling with their tactics.

A manipulator may also simply exist in your life to exploit your resources. They enter your life to enjoy the good things you have. They do feel jealous of you, but the idea is to make you share what you have. If you have a great start-up, they will present themselves as a valuable partner without even actually doing anything for your business. Similarly, if you are a successful independent person, a manipulator would decide to lure you into a relationship to share your life.

They just want what you have - a feeling, a physical item, a lifestyle or even your emotional control.

10. Self-centered

All characteristics come down to this one idea. Manipulators are self-centered. They do not understand or care about other people's thoughts, life, emotions or mental state. They only care about what they need. If people get hurt physically, emotionally or psychologically, it is all collateral. People are expendable if it fulfills some righteous purpose for a manipulator. That is how a manipulator sees the world. No matter how caring, logical and charming they sound, they don't mean a single word. It is all a formulated combination of words, emotions, and expressions to manipulate people and situations.

A manipulator can be surrounded by hundreds of people who love him/her and feel like a lone wolf in his mind, and this lone wolf is cold-hearted and ready to hunt no matter who or what comes in the way. Every situation is an opportunity to obtain something. If people are going through bad situations, manipulators find something to gain from it. They actually feel good and excited inside if bad things happen to other people because, in this way, they can use those vulnerable people.

The life of a manipulator is in his or her mind. They keep on plotting something in their mind. It is all a game to them, which is why they don't feel exhausted. Their personalities are rigid inside but they act all moral from the outside. This act of morality allows them to target other people's vulnerability and sense of morality too.

Now you know how to spot them, it gives you a better line of defense against such manipulative folk. Though it may seem harsh, but the line know an enemy and treat them as such resonates strongly here. You know how to identify manipulators, the next segment will equip you with the tools to deal with them.

CHAPTER 7 - Self-Defense Class 101

In nature, manipulative behavior is deceptive, sneaky and devious. Victims might feel a sense of uneasiness in some cases, but recognizing a manipulative situation seems difficult. Manipulators tend to alter victims' reality which makes them feel crazy but, while you are thinking it is all just your imagination, the manipulator is playing you.

Manipulators start learning and cultivating manipulative dysfunctional methods as children. Either they learn from the manipulative people around, or cultivate manipulative behavior to handle an authoritative parent. Twisting emotions and changing personality become the only way for them to get out of their miserable childhood but, eventually, the manipulation becomes a part of their personality and begins playing innocent people who are vulnerable.

Although there are hundreds of variations to every manipulative tactic, you can get an idea by going through the major ways of manipulation. Knowing how someone can try to manipulate you will allow you to immediately get yourself out of those situations.

Here is every manipulative situation with conversation examples that you can come across:

Using Group Affiliation to Borrow Strength

A manipulator can attack your morality, or gain superiority, by using group affiliation during communication:

1. *"As women, we desire/don't desire this from men."*

The power of a group is strong enough to put pressure on an individual. The group doesn't even have to be present physically. A manipulator can use a false sense of group affiliation to manipulate you. A manipulative woman can use sentences like this to shut you down.

For example:

If you are trying to show mistakes in a project to a female employee

A manipulative woman can try something like this, "Why are you being disrespectful? As women, all we ask is basic respect."

To this, most people back down, lower their voice and even stop the conversation. The idea is to divert the conversation by building a sense of guilt and shame in your heart.

To find a way out of this, you need to firmly stand your ground and choose words wisely.

You can say, "I am not disrespecting you, dear! I am talking to you exactly the way I would talk to any other male or female employee. As your senior, I have the right to point out your mistakes, and you should listen and learn from them."

2. "People, older than you, know better, so listen to me..."

These types of interactions happen when a manipulator is scared of your skills. If you have better skills or knowledge of something, an older manipulative person would cover his or her fear with arrogance.

Knowledgeable people pose threats to manipulators. To win arguments, or to shift the focus away from you, a manipulator tries to use his or her age as some sort of superiority. "I am better than you because I came to this planet before." That's what they are trying to convey. Sometimes, this technique is used to win control over your actions, or some elders try to hit your morality and respectful behavior with such conversations.

The age card is played in various scenarios, such as:

When a manipulative father wants his son to join the family business and stay under control

Son: "I think I'm going to join the environment care center in our town."

Father: "Why? We have our own seafood supply chain. Join our company. You will find me there to help you as I have been always."

Son: "I guess I'm ready to face the world now, dad!"

Father: "You see this white beard on my face?! I know this world better than you because I have been here longer. People don't waste time when they listen to their elders. You will be ready when I say you are."

Manipulative fathers try to keep their children near them. They have their personal agendas to fulfill.

To save yourself in a situation like this, say, "Dad! People become what they are because of the experiences they receive in life. I also want to become as experienced and wise as you are, but with my own wins and losses."

When your knowledge shines in a meeting in front of your older boss

You: "I think this AI should be our next step to get a competitive edge in the market. We don't have to begin right away. Just a little research in this direction would help our business."

A manipulative boss: "Well, I hear you, but people older than you have been managing this business for years so don't mind if I decide to not act right away on a young man's suggestion. In fact, I think AI is nothing but a stupid trend that would vanish away in a few years."

In such situations, you need to respond very politely. Don't let them convey that you are arrogant.

In a humble way, you can say, "I am not as old and experienced as you are, but I do have some skills that impressed you to hire me in the first place. I am just fulfilling the responsibility I was hired for. The ultimate decision is always yours. Just remember that it is my idea."

When your senior manipulates you to work overtime

You: "I have enough work for today. I will pick the rest of the work tomorrow."

Manipulative senior: "Buddy! I never act like your senior here, but you shouldn't forget that seniors know how things work. I have reached this position with hard work, just like other seniors you see in this office. I have done more overtime than you can even imagine. Believe me, today's hard work will help you tomorrow."

By using the seniority, the manipulator tries to build hope in your mind. Reluctantly, you decide to work overtime, and the cycle of overtimes starts from that day on.

To save yourself, you need to make your own decisions. Analyze whether you want to work late or not. Don't let your senior decide when and why you should work overtime against your will.

You can respond with something like this:

"Sir, I do understand the importance of hard work and I am following all my responsibilities here, but there is a life outside where I have more important responsibilities so I do have to prioritize. I am choosing other priorities today."

Generalizing Your Personality or Habits

A manipulator can try to label you to bring your value down:

1. "You are so stubborn"

Every time you want to stand your ground, manipulators shake you by saying that you are stubborn. They want to sell you their idea so, if you don't seem to buy their manipulation, they play the stubborn card. They confuse you into thinking that you aren't open to new ideas.

Friends, family members, lovers, or any manipulative person in your life can trick you like this. If you don't agree with what they say, you are a stubborn person.

If you observe closely, you will find manipulators using this tactic very often:

- **When a manipulative wife wants to move to the city where her parents live**

"My parents have found a great property for us there. We can start a new life. It will be an exciting start for us."

But husband says, *"Are you kidding? I have my friends, my job, and my family here."*

This forces to a situation something like this, *"Oh! You are such a stubborn guy. Move with the flow, my dad has a great post ready for you in his office."*

The wife desires her husband to move to her territory. This way, she will get better control of her husband. In fact, she can also control his career through her father.

Similar manipulative tactics are common in a girlfriend-boyfriend relationship and a parent-son or parent-daughter relationship as well.

To save yourself, you need to realize when you are being generalized. Anytime someone generalizes your decisions as a stubborn personality, shut them down.

"My decisions are driven by my own personal reasons. Don't generalize my decisions. I won't respond to those false accusations."

- **When you buy a car more expensive than your budget**

A manipulative salesman can push your buttons with this tactic. Sales professionals are taught tricks to play consumers; however, if a manipulative person becomes a salesman, he or she can make people buy things they don't even want.

You go out to buy an affordable car, but the salesman starts talking about the latest technologies and modern features.

"Sir, I am telling you, this car right here is what you need. People avoid technology due to stubbornness and end up facing consequences. This one is expensive, but it comes with better safety and comfort."

Whether you feel good about that car or not, afterwards, it is a different question. Don't let a salesman push the "stubborn" button and twist your decision. The wise move would be to start avoiding the salesman if he or she calls you stubborn directly or indirectly.

- **When a manipulative friend wants you to try something you don't want to do**

Friends can be really persuasive, especially if they have manipulative skills. A friend can make you try alcohol or make you do other things that you won't do generally, and it all happens due to the "stubborn" card.

"Just do it. We are all doing it. Why do you have to be so stubborn?"

Don't let this imprison you into doing a wrong thing.

"I am not stubborn. I don't want this right now."

If you stay firm with your decision, the manipulative friend will stop those efforts.

Similarly, you will find many situations where people will come and call you stubborn. Don't ignore them completely.

Not all of them are trying to manipulate you. Think and evaluate to make sure that all your decisions are yours only, and not forced.

2. "You always create drama..."

A manipulator can accuse you of overreacting to question your actions. This majorly happens if you get close to discovering a manipulator. They try to hide their actions by telling you that you are the one thinking too much and creating a drama over a small thing.

- **When you ask why your partner doesn't spend more time with you**

You: "You promised we will have dinner together this Sunday."

Manipulative partner: "Sorry, I have something important this Sunday."

You: "Why is it so difficult for you to find time for me? I see you spend time with all your friends."

Manipulative partner: "You are creating drama over nothing. I am working hard for our own future and everything is fine in our life. Stop making things up!"

The manipulator wants you to stop questioning.

If your partner accuses you of overreaction, you need to calm down first of all; then, make sure that your partner doesn't change the topic after that.

Say, "Don't try to stop this conversation like this. Give me valid reasons why things are going this way."

Also, you can include, *"Maybe I am overreacting, but it is because these things are important to me. Give me a legit answer for your behavior."*

- ## When a colleague tries to steal your limelight

You: "Why did you present that idea to the boss? I shared it with you in confidence."

Manipulative colleague: "Oh! Sorry man! I thought you were pitching that idea to me so I took the initiative of moving that idea forward."

You: "Are you kidding me? I clearly remember telling you not to say anything to anyone. I was waiting for the right time."

Manipulative colleague: "You were waiting for the right time! This is not a theatre man, it is a professional environment. I saw a moment and I pitched the idea. Stop creating drama over a small thing. Go tell the boss it was your idea if you want to."

You: "Not me. You should confess in front of the boss that it was my idea."

Manipulative colleague: "Such a drama every single time. What is wrong with you man? Calm down."

Manipulations like this leave you with a loss of many opportunities of growth in your career, and manipulative people get the promotions, which you deserve.

To save yourself, you need to learn to keep secrets. Do not share your ideas with a colleague just because he or she is friendly, talks to you, or brings gifts for you. A manipulator can disguise you into liking him or her and then get information from you. Secrets that don't harm anyone are not bad at all so there is nothing wrong with keeping your ideas to yourself, until you are ready to present it to the right authorities.

3. *"Why do you have to be the most negative person in the room?"*

The accusation of a being a negative person is embarrassing for everyone. No-one wants to be perceived as a negative personality but, sometimes, our concerns are presented as negativity, which doesn't allow us to convey our point. Manipulators do this to make our points of view worthless and make their ideas look positive.

- **If you stop fellow professionals from making a wrong business decision**

"I don't think we should move ahead with this plan. There are many variables associated with this. Things can easily go south."

Manipulators: *"Don't listen to this guy. He is always the most negative person in the room. Business is about risks and rewards so move forward with this plan."*

The manipulator tries to label you as a negative person. This way, other people in the room stop focusing on your point of view. Even if you present logical reasons, everything becomes an opinion of a negative and scared person.

To come out of such a situation, you need to present some positive decisions that you made before. Say, "I am not a negative person," and remind yourself of all those times when your decisions have been right. This manipulation affects multiple people, so you need to patiently react to win the trust of all those people.

After presenting your authority, you need to call the manipulator out, *"So, hopefully you now know about my decision-making abilities. I don't want you to call me a negative person ever. Keep your labels away from me."*

You can face similar accusations in your personal relationships as well. A manipulative partner can call you negative because you suspect he/she is cheating on you. In that situation, you should say, *"I am ready to hear your side, but don't accuse me just because I demand some answers."*

Always deal with patience and shut the manipulator's generalizations down. That's how you win over labeling.

Hooking You With Emotions

We all deal with one or many emotions on a daily basis. Emotions like pride, love, affection, guilt, and hope are a few of the major emotions that we all deal with every day. Manipulators can attack these emotions with certain hook lines. They know which statement will impact you exactly the way they want.

Knowing those emotional hooks can help you fight the temptation and charm of falling in the hole dug by manipulators.

1. *"You are my savior"*

Manipulators can act like a victim to gain sympathy. They call you their savior, which makes you feel like a hero. A little sense of pride is induced in your mind, which allows you to come forward whenever the manipulator is in need. The sympathy can also turn into trust. You don't feel that a person can harm you in any way, so you start sharing things. Eventually, the manipulator gains more control over your life and emotions.

- **When a person knows you have a crush on him/her**

"Every time I find myself alone, you come from somewhere to help me out. I have no money on me right now, so can you clear this bill for me please?"

You are already in 'awe' of that person, so you become ready to do everything to impress. They make you feel as if you are important, but you are nothing but a tool for those manipulative people.

- **When you are trying to impress your seniors in your workplace**

"There is no way I can complete this presentation on time. The work is out of control today. Then, I thought, where is my savior? I know you are the only one responsible enough to share this work I have."

A manipulative senior uses your sense of duty and presents himself as a victim of being a burdened employee. To this, you find yourself helping them every time and even feel good about it.

First of all, remind yourself every day that you don't need to impress anybody in this world. If you are responsible and follow your morals, don't let people turn you into their puppet.

When a person calls you his or her savior, judge the reasons behind it. Then, if you find signs of manipulation, break the conversation immediately with something like, *"I can't be a savior today. In fact, I need a savior right now with my work.*" If you can, add some legitimate work that you have to do immediately, and the manipulator would go away.

Manipulators never want to repay favors so, if you ask for it, they tend to leave. You can use this against their self-victimization tactic.

2. "I can share anything with you."

It is a famous tactic that manipulators use on their victims. They share fake emotional feelings so that you open your heart to them. If a manipulator says, "I can share anything with you," he or she tries to condition you to share your emotions and information with them. They want to know which emotions drive you as a person and what feelings you are currently dealing with so they create an emotional bond by saying this statement. Actually, a manipulator never shares his or her emotional state with others. Everything they say is just a fraction of their feelings, combined with fake scenarios.

- **In a new relationship with a manipulative partner**

Manipulator: *"I have never told these things about me to anyone before. You are so easy to talk to. I can share anything with you."*

You: *"Even I feel the same way."*

Have such a conversation two or three times, and you will end up sharing your emotions and other personal ideas that you never share with anyone. The manipulator will give you simple and fake information and call them his or her secrets. With these conversations, a manipulative partner finds your push buttons to control you in future.

To save yourself, you need to understand that if someone is sharing things, you don't have to do the same. Even if that person is your partner, decide the level of secrecy depending on the time you have spent with him/her. Never share your emotional weaknesses in the early stage of a relationship.

- **In a professional relationship**

Manipulators build professional relationships to gain information. They are generally eager to talk and share random information with conviction.

"I heard other teams have prepared their ideas for the project. My team hasn't even started yet, but I am telling this to you only. I know I can share these things with you."

"By the way, what's your plan for the project? Any ideas?"

Similar situations occur and you end up falling for this emotional hook in a professional environment. The solution is the same for this situation as well. You need to learn to keep your secrets yours only and to those you know you can trust. In a professional environment, all information has to be presented in front of the right person at the right moment. Keep this in mind and you will never fall for this manipulative tactic.

3. "Don't you feel any guilt because of that?"

The guilt trip is worse and a manipulator can further induce this feeling to control your actions. Some people are firm in their morality and try everything possible to stay righteous. It is a positive quality, but these are the people most prone to being manipulated with guilt. Manipulators can create scenarios with their dialogues and make you feel responsible for something bad.

Here are a few situations when manipulators can use this tactic on you:

- **An argument with a manipulative partner**

"Whenever we start becoming a perfect couple, you do something to mess things up for both of us. Don't you feel any guilt for your behavior?"

Or, something like this:

"I feel happy away from you and cry when I am with you. That's the effect you have on me. I hope you at least feel guilty."

Manipulative partners stir your emotions with such statements to shut you down. They don't want you to get out of their control so the guilt factor comes into play.

To save yourself, you need to have better control over your emotions. Don't allow your partner's statement to induce guilt in you. Feeling guilty is a positive emotion if you feel it on your own, but don't let other people decide when and why you should feel guilty.

You can reply, *"I am not doing anything deliberately. I still apologize if you are feeling bad, but I am not guilty of anything."*

- **A manipulative relative decides you stir emotions during a family gathering**

"Your parents always treated me with respect and you do not even care to call me even on festivals. You are ruining the reputation your parents built. You should think about it before it's too late."

In such a situation, you can't turn things towards the manipulator. The only way you can win is by not allowing that guilt trip attack your integrity. Respectfully reply:

"I respect my elders and my parents know that."

Family members use such tactics for no reason sometimes. Their goal is to stir things and enjoy people feeling bad. If you start explaining things too much, it would make them happier. In fact, they will further manipulate you into doing things for them so stop the conversation as quickly as possible and don't feel bad because someone has said something.

4. "You are perfect, just change this one thing."

We all hope to become the best version of ourselves. We want to be a better person, a better partner, a better professional and gain other improvements. This hope also becomes a method of manipulation for manipulators. They often come into your life as well-wishers, motivators, teachers and other personalities you look up to. Even your partner can use your hopes to control you.

Manipulators want to control your actions so they give compliments first to make you feel good. Eventually, they start seeding ideas of changes that would make you better. As you become addicted to their approval, you follow through and act exactly the way manipulators want.

Such manipulations occur in families, relationships, and work as well:

- **Your parents ask you to leave your partner because he/she is a bad influence**

126

Manipulative parents condition their kids with their manipulation. Kids grow up, but the habit of manipulation doesn't go away in parents. They try to control the kid's actions.

Suppose manipulative parents see their son getting freedom from their manipulation because of a new partner in his life. They would say:

"You have a perfect life with us and now things are changing because of this new girl. This change will ruin your life. Just get away from this girl and you will become our perfect child again."

There are parents with manipulative behavior. They don't want their kids to get out of their control, and that can make things ugly for the child, especially if the child has a caring and responsible nature.

If you are going through something like this, realization is the first step towards the solution. Your childhood conditioning might not allow you to see the manipulation coming from your parents; hence, you need to start thinking and making decisions on your own. Take suggestions from your parents for sure, but don't allow them to make decisions or emotionally blackmail you.

Similarly:

- **A manipulative partner can ask you to change your behavior**

"Why are you again asking about shopping bills? You are a perfect boyfriend. Just stop asking questions that I don't like. I have the right to spend your money as I wish."

Not cute, right, but it happens a lot. Both girls and guys can fall into such manipulative relationship traps.

Breaking such manipulation comes down to how confident you are as a person. Low self-esteem and seeking approval allows manipulators to use this tactic on you. A partner won't behave the same way if you show self-confidence.

"We both have our own identities. My money is my money and I decide whether you get it or if you don't. If that defines my love, you don't love me at all."

You can choose your own words, but make sure that the partner sees your confident side.

- **There is always some lame reason why you are denied promotion**

Unfortunately, workplaces have become a hub to manipulate and use vulnerable people. Your vulnerability is tested by your seniors but, instead of saving you from those vulnerabilities, manipulative people use them to their advantage.

No matter how hardworking you are, your promotion goes to the next person who doesn't even deserve it and you get one silly reason:

"Your work is great. Just listen to your seniors more to learn and prepare for the position you are aspiring to attain in this company."

Less-deserving people will keep getting promotions unless you stand up for yourself. The first step would be to ensure that your work performance is top-notch. Others will try to point out strange and irrelevant mistakes. You have to learn to defend your work. Use facts to describe your professional work and decisions.

Then, stand up for yourself and ask for a promotion. This way, your seniors will understand your importance and won't get to steal away your promotion.

Conclusion

You can bring down everything to one idea - **Learn to understand, control and protect your emotions and psychology.**

Manipulators are out there learning vulnerabilities. To fight them, you need to understand your vulnerabilities and resolve them. The more you understand your inner-self, the stronger personality you attain.

Also, when you come across a manipulative personality, try to walk away as quickly as possible. Use the tips and ideas given in this book to read the signs of a manipulative situation. Face such situations with integrity, and don't let a manipulator enter your emotional and psychological space.

Hopefully, reading about manipulation will help you improve your life, and allow you to fight people who are out there to just use you one way or the other.

Now, I would like to make a small request again.

If you have enjoyed or found even one piece of advice useful in your daily life, would you please share with others by leaving your review on amazon.

This will mean loads to me as well as the folks who read it such that they know how you have benefited from this book.

Many thanks once again!

Catch you around and meanwhile don't forget to practice the skills and strategies taught therein so that you can lessen and avoid the impact of manipulation in your life!

60833898R00081

Made in the USA
Columbia, SC
18 June 2019